THE STARS OF SHOW JUMPING

THE STARS
OF
SHOW JUMPING

JUDITH DRAPER

STANLEY PAUL
London Sydney Auckland Johannesburg

Stanley Paul & Co. Ltd

An imprint of the Random Century Group
Random Century House, 20 Vauxhall Bridge Road,
London SW1V 2SA

Random Century Australia (Pty) Ltd
20 Alfred Street, Milsons Point, Sydney, NSW 2061

Random Century New Zealand Limited
191 Archers Road, PO Box 40-086, Glenfield, Auckland 10

Century Hutchinson South Africa (Pty) Ltd
PO Box 337, Bergvlei 2012, South Africa

First published 1990

Copyright © Judith Draper, 1990

Typeset in Linotronic Baskerville by
SX Composing Ltd, Rayleigh, Essex

Printed and bound by Toppan, Singapore

British Library Cataloguing in Publication Data
is available upon request from the British Library

ISBN 0 09 174521 7

*The author and publishers would like to thank the following for
allowing the reproduction of copyright photographs*

p.1 and p.3 (Bob Langrish)
John Whitaker p.7, p.9, p.10 (Bob Langrish); p.11
(Elizabeth Furth)
Michael Whitaker p.12, p.17 (Elizabeth Furth); p.14, p.15,
p.16 (Bob Langrish)
Nick Skelton p. 18 (Elizabeth Furth); p.19, p.21, p.22-3,
p.23 (Bob Langrish)
Joe Turi p.24, p.25, p.28 (Bob Langrish); p.26, p.27 (Jan
Gyllensten); p.29 (AllSport)
David Broome p.30, p.31 (Kit Houghton); p.32 (Bob
Langrish); p.33 (Leslie Lane); p.34-5 (S & G Press
Agency)
Liz Edgar p.36, p.37, p.39, p.40 (Bob Langrish)
Pierre Durand p.42 (Kit Houghton); p.43 (Elizabeth
Furth); p.44 (Jan Gyllensten); p.45 (Bob Langrish)
Ian Millar p.46, p.48-9 (Bob Langrish); p.50-1 (Jan
Gyllensten)
Franke Sloothaak p.53 (Elizabeth Furth); p.54, p.55 (Bob
Langrish); p.56 (Jan Gyllensten)
Thomas Frühmann p.59 (Kit Houghton); p.60, p.62, p.63
(Elizabeth Furth)
Malcolm Pyrah p.64, p.66, p.67 (Bob Langrish)

The Americans p.68, p.71, p.72, p.73 (below) (Elizabeth
Furth); p.68-9 (Jan Gyllensten); p.70-1, p.73 (above),
p.74, p.75, p.77 (Bob Langrish); p.76 (Kit Houghton)
Emma-Jane Mac p.78 (Kit Houghton); p.79, p.80-1 (Bob
Langrish)
Harvey Smith p.82, p.83, p.84 (Bob Langrish); p.85 (S & G
Press Agency)
Robert Smith p.86, p.87 (Bob Langrish); p.88 (Elizabeth
Furth); p.89 (Jan Gyllensten)
Steven Smith p.90 (Elizabeth Furth); p.91 (Kit Houghton)
Nelson Pessoa p.94 (Elizabeth Furth); p.95 (Findlay
Davidson)
Eddie Macken p.99 (Kit Houghton); p.101 (Richard Earle);
p.102, p.103 (Bob Langrish)
Annette Miller p.104-5 (Bob Langrish); p.107 (Jan
Gyllensten)
Philip Heffer p.109, p.110 (Bob Langrish); p.111 (Jan
Gyllensten)
Hugo Simon p.112, p.114, p.115 (above), p.117 (Bob
Langrish); p.113, p.115 (below), p.116 (Jan Gyllensten)
Peter Murphy p.118, p.122 (Elizabeth Furth); p.121 (Bob
Langrish)
Marie Edgar p.124, p.127 (Kit Houghton)

Contents

John Whitaker

Above: *John Whitaker and Ryan's Son at Hickstead in 1985. Ryan put up some of his best performances at the Sussex showground, winning the Derby there in 1983*

Milton jumping in typically exuberant style during the 1989 Hickstead Nations Cup, not long before winning the European Championship in Rotterdam

Q UIETLY SPOKEN, MODEST AND UNASSUMING, John Whitaker is the antithesis of most people's idea of the typical Yorkshireman. Born on 5 August 1955 into a farming family in the west of the county, he has risen to the top of the show jumping tree untouched by scandal or controversy. His delightful sense of humour, not to mention his mastery of the art of understatement, has made him one of the most popular riders on the circuit.

Like his three younger brothers, Steven, Michael and Ian, John was taught to ride by his mother, Enid, who showed him the basic skills and then encouraged him to go out and learn by experience. He rode a lot in gymkhanas and, as a member of the Pony Club, developed his all-round horsemanship skills.

Expensive ponies were out of the question for the Whitakers, and anyway John's father, Donald, with his farming background, preferred to see horses earning their keep in harness, not being kept for fun. Indeed, John's first mare, Peggy, had spent most of her life between the shafts; and his first good jumper, Bonnie, cost a mere £20. John's ability to get the best out of mediocre partners did not go unnoticed, and when he came to make the problematical change from ponies to adult jumping, people soon

7

began sending him horses to ride. In fact, horses have always tended to come to him. Among them have been two of the best in the world: Ryan's Son and Milton.

Ryan's Son, with his plain white face, feet the size of dinner plates and exuberant kick-back, was to become one of the best-loved horses in show-jumping history. But although Donald Whitaker liked him at first sight, John was not attracted, describing him as 'funny-looking'. However, he soon changed his mind when the gelding's then owner, Donald Oates, asked John to jump him in some novice classes. Whatever he looked like, this was evidently a horse with great potential.

Because he could not afford the asking price for Ryan, Donald Whitaker decided to approach businessman Malcolm Barr who was looking for a nice horse for John to ride. Mr Barr's interest in horses stemmed from that of his daughters, Clare and Janine, friends of John's on the show circuit. He had sent his ex-hunter Rufus the Red to John to try out as a jumper, and John had had a successful season with him in 1972 before the horse was sold on. Mr Barr agreed to buy Ryan.

This link with Malcolm Barr was to determine John's future in more ways than one. Ryan's Son made him an international star. And in 1979 Clare Barr, who had gone to work at the Whitakers' yard in 1974, became his wife. John lost no time in learning to cope with the headstrong but immensely talented five-year-old Ryan. In early 1974 he upgraded him to A and was soon competing alongside the established stars of the sport. During the following season the pair made their Nations Cup debut with the British team and in 1976, having won one Olympic trial and been placed in two others, in addition to going exceptionally well at the Royal International and at shows abroad, they looked lively contenders for a place in the squad for the Montreal Games.

The selectors indicated that Ryan should be put on the easy list in readiness. But later, and quite unexpectedly, another trial was organised at Hickstead. Now Ryan's one flaw, which was more pronounced in his younger days, was that after a lay-off he would behave 'like a lunatic', as John puts it, when he returned to the showring. So it was that fateful day at Hickstead. After being rushed down to the final trial he committed just about every sin in the book, including refusing, and was dismissed by the selectors.

With the knowledge of hindsight, his omission from those exceptionally tough Olympics could well have been a blessing in disguise. The courses in Montreal were big, the ground conditions terrible for the individual final, and Ryan, then only an eight-year-old, might well have had fewer years at the top if he had been subjected to such a test at that stage in his career.

As it was, his career very nearly came to a permanent end a

The Whitaker brothers, Michael (left) *and John, in pensive mood on the victory podium at the 1989 European Championships*

couple of years later when he was brought up from grass slightly lame in his offhind and was found to have broken a piece off the pedal bone in his foot, presumably by stepping on something sharp. An operation under general anaesthetic was unavoidable. Fortunately, Ryan made a complete recovery. 'It's a good job he's got big feet,' John joked afterwards. 'There was plenty to operate on!' He and Clare still have the sliver of bone preserved in a jar.

After a lengthy rest Ryan returned to competition as good as new. In 1979 he finished equal fifth in the first running of the World Cup and by 1980 was an obvious choice for the Moscow Olympic team. But once again John was to be disappointed. Britain decided to boycott the Games because of the Soviet invasion of Afghanistan. There was, however, the consolation of the International Show Jumping Festival at Rotterdam, organised by the FEI for all those teams who had not gone to Moscow, which in effect meant every top jumping nation in the world.

John and Ryan were duly selected as members of the four-man team which, in keeping with the true Olympic spirit, was made up totally of amateurs. It was every bit a championship, over courses which John says were the biggest he has ever jumped. He and Ryan helped the team to win the silver medal in the Nations Cup, collecting only 4 faults in the two rounds, and on the final day won another silver in the individual contest.

It was the beginning of non-stop championship appearances for John. After finishing equal third in the 1982 World Cup, he won a team bronze in that year's World Championships in Dublin and the following year won team and individual silver in the Europeans at Hickstead, all with Ryan's Son. The next year Ryan, at the age of sixteen, jumped a crucial final round in Los Angeles to give John his long wished-for and much-deserved first Olympic medal, a team silver. In 1985 John won a team gold and the individual bronze in the European Championships in Dinard, and twelve months later a team silver in the World Championships at Aachen, both times with Hopscotch. That same year Ryan's Son capped his wonderful career by winning the coveted and historic King George V Gold Cup at the Royal International Horse Show.

No rider's career is untouched by tragedy, and the biggest blow of John's competitive life came on 2 August 1987. Ryan's Son, still fit and well at the age of nineteen but competing on a much-reduced scale just to give him an interest in his old age, took a crashing fall at the second fence in the Hickstead Derby and a few hours later collapsed and died. A post mortem revealed haemorrhaging into the chest and the structure around the heart, associated with severe bruising to the chest muscles caused by his fall. It was particularly ironic that his end should have come at Hickstead, the course which suited his style of jumping so well and where he had won the Derby (in 1983) and three times finished runner-up (in 1980, 1981 and 1985).

Fortunately for John, fate had meanwhile already brought him an even more outstanding horse in the form of Milton, the grey gelding of whom the late Caroline Bradley had thought so highly and whom her parents, Tom and Doreen, had given John to ride in 1985. Success was instantaneous: the Calgary Grand Prix (the world's richest prize) in 1986; team gold and individual silver in the 1987 Europeans in St Gallen; a host of Grands Prix and Nations Cup successes in 1988, when John missed out on the Olympics yet again, this time because of the reluctance of Milton's owners to risk sending him to Seoul; runner-up in the 1989 World Cup and, a few months later, victory in the European Championship in Rotterdam and another team gold. In April 1990 John and Milton became the first Europeans since 1979, and the first ever British pair to win the World Cup.

All this success has changed John not a whit. He still gets nervous before a big class; he is still as quiet and unobtrusive as ever; he has never lost his gentle sense of humour. His answer to a question put by an earnest foreign journalist after one big championship has become a legend among the equestrian press. Asked if there was a big difference between Ryan's Son and Milton, he contemplated for a few moments and then said, apparently in all seriousness, 'Ay, colour.'

His considerable talents include some not evident to those watching from the stands. One is his ability to sleep anywhere at any time – in taxis, at crowded airports, in a horsebox full of noisy young children. For someone whose travel schedule is, to put it mildly, hectic, it is a wonderful gift. So, too, is his ability to stay cool under pressure. One outstanding example of this was in December 1988 when his plane to the Bordeaux World Cup show was delayed for several hours. He and the other British riders were still actually on the plane when the first class was beginning. Met by car, and given special permission to jump last should they arrive in time, they duly reached the showground just as the last few competitors were jumping. John calmly stepped into the riding clothes proffered by his groom, climbed aboard San Salvador and went out and won the class.

His prowess for competing in two shows in different countries at the same time is also legendary. He brought it to a fine art in 1989 when he commuted between the Royal International in Birmingham and the Aachen international show, where he helped Britain win the Nations Cup. During Olympia later that year he took time off to go to Grenoble for the final of the Renault Jump Series. Arriving back in London halfway through the big class he calmly won it, just as in Bordeaux, without walking the course.

John and Hopscotch competing in Dinard, where they won team gold and individual bronze medals in the 1985 European Championships

No wonder, then, that when Henderson Unit Trust Management came up with the biggest sponsorship deal in British show-jumping history – £1.5 million over three years – at the end of 1989, it was John and his brother Michael who were the chief beneficiaries. They could not have entered into their first sports venture with a more talented, more popular and less temperamental duo.

In spite of his world-wide travels, John has never abandoned his Yorkshire roots. He and Clare live on a farm at Upper Cumberworth, high on the hills in the west of the county. Their partnership has been one of the most successful in the sport. With the eldest of their three children, Louise, already competing in pony jumping, and the two younger ones, Robert and Joanne, waiting in the wings, the future of the Whitaker dynasty looks assured.

Career Highlights

Milton showing the supreme athleticism that made him arguably the greatest show jumper of the late eighties

1976 National Champion (Ryan's Son)
1980 International Show Jumping Festival, Rotterdam, team and individual silver medals (Ryan's Son)
1982 World Championships, team bronze medal (Ryan's Son)
      World Cup, equal third place (Ryan's Son)
1983 European Championships, team and individual silver medals (Ryan's Son)
      World Cup European League, winner
      Hickstead Derby (Ryan's Son)
1984 Olympic Games, team silver medal (Ryan's Son)
1985 European Championships, team gold and individual bronze medals (Hopscotch)
1986 World Championships, team silver medal (Hopscotch)
      World Cup European League, third place
      King George V Gold Cup (Ryan's Son)
1987 European Championships, team gold and individual silver medals (Milton)
      World Cup European League, second place
1989 European Championships, team and individual gold medals (Milton)
      World Cup, second place (Milton)
1990 World Cup European League, winner
      World Cup, winner (Milton)

11

Michael Whitaker

Above: *A triumphant moment for Michael Whitaker: victory on Monsanta in the du Maurier International, the world's richest Grand Prix*

Michael and the talented but sometimes capricious mare Amanda jumping in Rome

MICHAEL WHITAKER, BROTHER OF JOHN and his junior by five years, has never had a horse of Milton's calibre to ride, but he is not one to let that stand between him and success on the international circuit. He rides with such tremendous flair and determination that he inspires horses who are perhaps not quite top class to perform as if they are outstanding. He has twice come within an ace of beating the world at championship level, and the fates will be unkind indeed if he does not soon claim a major title.

The third son of Enid and Donald Whitaker, Michael was born in Yorkshire on 17 March 1960 and today lives with his Belgian-born wife Véronique (née Daems-Vastapane) in the wilds of the Pennines on the Cheshire/Derbyshire border. Like his brothers he was taught to ride by his mother, and from the moment when he helped Britain to win the team bronze in the 1976 Junior European Championships and then, two years later, the team gold with a brilliant double clear on Brother Scott, it was obvious that he was going right to the top of the sport.

An incredibly versatile rider, Michael can establish a rapport with any horse apparently overnight, something which is reflected in the number of big classes he has won on a wide variety of different mounts. In 1989 at the Royal International Horse Show, he

13

had to ride his Puissance specialist Next Didi in the big classes after his Grand Prix horse was laid off with pulled back muscles. Michael astonished everyone by defeating his brother, who was riding Milton, in a jump-off against the clock for the King George V Gold Cup. Two days later he won the Grand Prix on the same horse.

Michael had first hit the headlines in senior competition when he became, at twenty, the youngest ever winner of the gruelling Hickstead Derby in 1980. His partner was Mr and Mrs Raymond Fenwick's Owen Gregory, and they jumped a magnificent clear round. Owen Gregory was to come out year after year at Hickstead and go well in the Derby. In his old age he spent most of his time on his owners' farm and would be reunited with Michael only shortly before an event, but the partnership always looked as smoothly oiled as if there had been no interruption.

Michael had a brilliant 1982 season with Mr Samiar Mahmoud's Disney Way, winner of both the King George V Gold Cup and the Grand Prix at the Royal International and top money winner for the year in national competitions. Although Michael had begun to represent his country in senior Nations Cup teams only that year, by 1984 there was little doubt that he would be in the Olympic squad for Los Angeles. The joint sponsorship that Michael and John had obtained enabled them, unlike most of the other top British riders, to remain amateurs, and even with only a couple of years' senior experience behind him, Michael had proved himself a valuable asset on any team.

With his cool, positive approach he was a natural choice to go as first man in the Los Angeles Nations Cup, where his partner was the enigmatic Amanda, a mare with boundless talent but with an unfortunate 'thing' about water ditches. At one time careful schooling seemed to have cured her but, as she was to demonstrate again later in her career, you could never be quite sure. In the Los Angeles team event, however, she was on her best behaviour, and followed a good first round (only 8 faults) with a brilliant second effort, one of only ten clears in the whole contest. It came at a vital time for Britain and helped to clinch the silver medal.

In the first round of the individual championship, over a typically testing de Nemethy course, Michael conjured another clear round out of the mare. Only one other rider emulated him – Joe Fargis on his mare Touch of Class. At the halfway stage, therefore, Michael was in line for a medal. But the second-round course was to prove a disaster, with its treble comprising a wall and two spreads over water ditches. The wall prevented Amanda from seeing the first water ditch until she was in mid-air, and Michael felt her 'freeze' under him as she caught sight of it. Back-

Michael with Monsanta during the 1989 European Championships, where they so nearly won the individual title

Michael and Warren Point competing at Aachen, where they helped Britain win the team silver medal in the 1986 World Championships

ing off all the way she ground to a halt at the second ditch, and although he got her through the combination at the second attempt, his score had shot up to 28.50 faults and all hopes of a placing had evaporated.

Following this biggest disappointment of his career, there was some consolation the following season when he won a team gold in his first senior European Championships on the excitable Warren Point, who always went so well for him. He followed this with a team silver in the 1986 World Championships with the same horse, and in 1987 renewed his partnership with Amanda to win a second European gold, though the mare was not on her best form and did not contribute materially to the team's victory.

In 1988 Amanda was again Michael's chief hope for the Olympics, but at the final trial in Dublin she once again misbehaved at those dreaded water ditches, and although she went to Seoul she was eventually left out of the team. To have a rider of Michael's calibre on the sidelines for lack of horsepower was clearly ridiculous, and there and then David Broome's long-time friend and backer Sir Phil Harris resolved to do something about it. It was decided that Monsanta, the horse with whom Gillian Greenwood had been enjoying such success, should be acquired for Michael to ride. The deal was struck, and by the time the 1989 European Championships in Rotterdam came round, the pair, having been together for only a few months, already had the makings of a fearsome duo.

John and Milton went to Rotterdam as favourites to depose the reigning champions, Pierre Durand and Jappeloup. But Michael was not going to hand it to his brother on a plate, and after finishing ninth in the opening speed leg he produced the only double clear round of the Nations Cup to secure most emphatically a third team gold medal and to go into the individual final actually ahead of Milton. Not since the days of the Italian d'Inzeo brothers had Europe seen such a battle between two equally gifted siblings. Michael and Monsanta held on to their lead through the first round of the final leg, and for the second time in a major championship Michael found himself in with a chance of a gold medal.

But Milton seemed to be going better and better the more fences he jumped. When he finished his final round he was less than a fence behind Monsanta, leaving Michael, who was last of all to go, needing another clear to take the individual title. So friendly is the rivalry between the two Whitakers that John, standing at the ringside, was torn between wanting to win himself and not wanting to see his brother have a fence down. Alas, there was to be no fairy-tale ending for Michael. Monsanta, perhaps tiring after his magnificent effort in the Nations Cup two days earlier, touched the fourth fence and faulted at the next, and

Michael saw gold change to silver in a few brief seconds. No one who witnessed it, though, will ever forget the extraordinary way in which this brilliant new combination had fought to the line in an effort to beat arguably the best horse in the world. Only once before in the history of show jumping had two brothers taken gold and silver in the same championship – those celebrated d'Inzeos in the Rome Olympics of 1960.

Again, and typical of the ups and downs of the sport, there was some compensation for Michael not long afterwards when he rode Monsanta to victory in the world's richest Grand Prix, the du Maurier International in Calgary, worth £82,500 to the winner. Monsanta jumped a triple clear. John and Milton failed to get into the jump-off.

The delightful thing about the Whitakers is that they do not just seem to be good friends, they genuinely are. Even when they were boys their rivalry was amicable – 'With five years between us there was never any need to fight over the same ponies,' Michael explains – and nothing has happened to change that friendly competitiveness. Nowadays, even when it comes to high-powered sponsorship, they still prefer to stay together as a team – though they operate from two quite separate yards.

Unusually for a leading rider, Michael is married to someone who still competes. Véronique was a highly successful junior international, winning a team gold for Belgium in the Junior Europeans of 1975 and twice taking individual silver. Since marrying Michael in December 1980 she has continued to ride internationally, notably with Jingo and Cogshall Spot On. In 1984 she became the first Belgian-born rider to win the Queen Elizabeth II Cup at the Royal International (though she was officially representing Great Britain), and she still enjoys the cut and thrust of international competition.

Disney Way, the horse on whom Michael won his first King George V Gold Cup in 1982

The 1980 Hickstead Derby winner Owen Gregory

Career Highlights

1976   Junior European Championships, team bronze medal
       (Bericote Cappucino)
1978   Junior European Championships, team gold medal
       (Brother Scott)
1980   Hickstead Derby (Owen Gregory)
1982   King George V Gold Cup (Disney Way)
1984   Olympic Games, team silver medal (Amanda)
       National Champion (Amanda)
1985   European Championships, team gold medal (Warren
       Point)
1986   World Championships, team silver medal (Warren
       Point)
1987   European Championships, team gold medal (Amanda)
1989   European Championships, team gold and individual
       silver medals (Monsanta)
       King George V Gold Cup (Didi)

Michael's skill at swiftly forming a rapport with a new horse was well demonstrated when he took over the ride on Monsanta, seen here at Hickstead

Nick Skelton

Above: Apollo, the horse on whom Nick Skelton won a clutch of Championship medals during the late eighties

Nick and the ill-fated J Nick step neatly down the massive Hickstead Derby bank on their way to victory in 1987

WHEN NICK SKELTON TOOK HIS PONY over to Liz and Ted Edgar's for schooling during the summer of 1973, he had no thoughts of taking up show jumping professionally. Born on 30 December 1957, Nick was fifteen years old at the time and with all the conviction of youth had set his heart on becoming a National Hunt jockey. Although he enjoyed doing some junior jumping, he much preferred to watch racing on television and then go out and gallop his pony round the field with his knees under his chin, in an attempt to emulate the stars of the winter game.

That visit to the Edgars was to change the course of his life. They suggested to Nick's father, a Warwickshire chemist, that Nick should try some jumping with them during the summer of 1974 after he left school. He left in the April at the instigation of his headmaster, who had deduced that his 'outdoor activities' were more important to him than academic studies. Nick, a trifle reluctantly, took up the Edgars' offer. It was not long before he was totally bitten by the jumping bug.

Nick learned the business the hard way, mostly riding novices. Among them was the aptly named Maybe, a horse with a wonderful jump but a difficult disposition. His inclination to nap (refuse to jump) meant that he could never be totally relied upon, but on his good days he was so very good that he quickly became a great favourite with his young rider. In his first year with the Edgars Nick helped the British team to win a silver medal in the Junior European Championships in Lucerne and went on to take the Whitbread Young Riders' competition at the Horse of the Year Show, on both occasions riding Maybe.

Nick was more than a little disconcerted when, the following year, Sir Hugh Fraser decided to buy Maybe for his wife Aileen to ride. He need not have worried. Maybe soon demonstrated the error of his ways, refusing even to go through the start at a show in Scotland, and in no time at all he was returned to the Edgars. Nick was selected to ride in the Junior Europeans again that year, but because of Maybe's unpredictability Ted suggested he ride OK, who had come from the yard of the Belgian dealer François Mathy. OK may not have been the most careful of jumpers but he had none of Maybe's unreliability, and Nick duly won the individual Junior European title with him in Dornbirn, Austria, as well as another team silver.

At the end of 1978, the year during which he rode in his first senior Nations Cup team, Nick quite literally hit the heights by breaking the British high-jump record at Olympia. He had taken over the ride on the grey Lastic when Ted broke his leg during the summer. After Lastic won the Olympia Puissance, an attempt was made to break the record of 7ft 6¼in (2.29 metres) set in the same arena back in 1937 by Donald Beard on Swank.

In a high-jump competition there is one specially designed fence of sloping poles, constructed so as to minimise the likelihood of damage to the horse, and competitors have three attempts at each height. The huge fence was set at 7ft 7⁵⁄₁₆in (2.32 metres) and Nick did not have any great hopes of clearing it. Lastic failed at his first two attempts, demolishing the whole structure at his second attempt and giving both himself and his rider a fright. But at his last try Lastic pulled out all the stops and, despite bouncing a pole, landed with the fence still intact. Photographs of this historic occasion show Lastic's young jockey looking down in astonishment as the horse clears the top pole.

Despite his successes, during those early years there were times when Nick would fall out with Ted and go back to his nearby home, only to rejoin the Edgar fold a few days later. In all he spent a valuable twelve years with Liz and Ted, absorbing all they could teach him and establishing himself as one of the top riders in the world.

His first big senior championship success came in 1980 at the International Festival ('alternative Olympics') in Rotterdam, where Maybe rewarded Nick's loyalty by winning a team silver, jumping one of only three double clear rounds. Since then Nick

St James, leading British money winner in 1984-85

Below right: Near disaster as Lastic drops his legs in the huge fence during his second attempt on the high-jump record

Nick and Lastic clear 7ft 7⁵/₁₆in (2.32 metres) at Olympia in 1978 to set a new British high-jump record

has been one of the most consistently reliable members of the British team, winning a team bronze at the 1982 World Championships on If Ever, team gold on St James in the 1985 Europeans, team silver and individual bronze in the 1986 World Championships with Apollo, team gold again and individual bronze in the 1987 Europeans, and in 1989 a third European team gold, all with Apollo.

Having decided to turn professional in 1982 to enable the horses he rode to carry the Edgars' Everest prefix, he was not available for the Los Angeles Olympics, but by the time of the Seoul Games in 1988 he had successfully re-applied for 'competitor' status and was selected for the team with Apollo, who finished equal seventh individually.

It was Mrs Linda Jones's big bay gelding Apollo who, during the second half of the eighties, filled the role of Nick's most outstanding ride after the retirement of the brilliant St James. Ted Edgar had bought St James from his brother-in-law David Broome in 1981 for owner Terry Clemence. Formerly known as Sunny Side Up and then Harris Home Care, the Irish-bred gelding was given the vastly more memorable name of St James and quickly became Nick's number-one partner. A remarkable run of successes in early 1981 led to a victory in the National Championship and then at the Royal International, after a narrow defeat in the King George V Gold Cup, success in the John Player Grand Prix and the Everest Supreme Championship, and leading horse and rider of the show awards.

Nick's partnership with St James was not, however, without its interruptions. Sarah-Jane, daughter of the horse's owner Terry Clemence, was in Young Riders at the time and wished to com-

pete with St James herself. Being a strong ride, St James on occasion proved too much for her and began to put in the occasional
stop when he found himself not exactly right at a fence. He would
go back to Nick for a while, then be returned for Sarah-Jane to
ride, and it was an unsettling time for all concerned.

However, when they were together and Nick had sorted out the
stopping problem, St James was quite brilliant. The pair won the
Grand Prix at Olympia two years running (1982–83) as well as the
1984 King George V Gold Cup. At the Horse of the Year Show in
October that year Nick hit an unbelievable winning streak, taking
no fewer than ten classes – two with St James, four with Everest
Radius, two with the Earl of Inchcape's Halo, one with his new
ride Apollo, and the champion horseman, a class in which the
leading four riders compete on four borrowed horses.

In 1985 Nick and St James came nearer than any other British
rider of the eighties to winning the elusive World Cup final. Held
in Berlin, it developed into a battle royal between the American
Conrad Homfeld, with his Olympic horse Abdullah, and Nick
with St James. Nick needed to go clear in the second round of the
final leg to pip Homfeld, but a mistake close to home robbed him
of victory by just one fault.

At the end of that year Nick took the biggest step of his career
when he decided to leave the Edgars. By this time he was married
to fellow show jumper Sarah Edwards, and the couple decided to
set up their own yard at the nearby Warwickshire village of Lowsonford, where they and their young sons are still based. (Incidentally, Nick's love of racing obviously dies hard. Sarah once
revealed that he was intent on naming the first of his two sons
'Lester'. 'Lester Skelton? What happens if he doesn't even *like*
horses?' Sarah made up her mind that she would get to choose his
name. She won. He is called Daniel.)

After the move to Lowsonford, Nick continued to ride St James,
leading British money winner of 1984 and 1985, for his new sponsors, Raffles, and by the time that horse eventually retired at the
end of 1986 he had established a marvellous partnership with
Apollo, previously the mount of Geoff Glazzard. Apollo became a
terrific Grand Prix horse, taking Nick to many international successes in the late eighties. And as the Seoul Olympic year
approached, Nick looked to have as strong a hand as anyone as far
as horsepower was concerned. In August 1987 he won the Hickstead Derby in fine style on Mrs Joyce Elliott's bold, brave horse J
Nick, who vied with Apollo as the top horse in the Skeltons' yard.

But so often when misfortunes come they come in battalions,
and when Airborne, the horse Nick was riding for former international Sally Mapleson, died following an operation for twisted
gut not long after Wembley 1987, it heralded two more major

*Nick and Gail Greenough's horse Mr
T in a spot of bother during the
change-horse final of the 1986 World
Championships. Nick finished third*

blows. Raffles announced that they would not be renewing their sponsorship in 1988, and, worse, in May that year at a show in France, a freak accident robbed Nick of the talented J Nick. Landing over the last fence in a competition, J Nick struck into a foreleg with such force that he all but severed the foot above the pedal bone, and although he was rushed to a leading equine clinic in Belgium, nothing could be done to save him and he had to be put down. Nick was reduced to one top horse and no sponsor.

However, a decade in international show jumping had left 'Skelly', as he is known on the circuit, anything but ill-equipped to fight back from such adversity. By the beginning of 1989 his horses were sporting a new prefix and he had some more than useful performers backing up Apollo. Early 1990 saw Nick again sponsorless and with some of his best up and coming horses for sale, but he was riding in such tremendous form that it seemed unlikely he would remain without backing for long. Apollo excelled himself by winning the Hickstead Derby in the two years following his ill-fated stable companion's victory, making Nick the first British rider to score a hat-trick in successive years in this marathon contest.

Career Highlights

Nick with Maybe, one of the Warwickshire rider's most outstanding partners during his early days with the Edgars

1974 Junior European Championships, team silver medal (Maybe)
1975 Junior European Championships, individual gold medal (OK)
1978 British High Jump Record (Lastic)
1980 International Show Jumping Festival, Rotterdam, team silver medal (Maybe)
1981 National Champion (St James)
1982 World Championships, team bronze medal (If Ever)
1983 World Cup European League, second place
1984 World Cup European League, winner
King George V Gold Cup (St James)
1985 European Championships, team gold medal (St James)
Word Cup, second place (St James)
1986 World Championships, team silver and individual bronze medals (Apollo)
World Cup European League, winner
1987 European Championships, team gold and individual bronze medals (Apollo)
1989 European Championships, team gold medal (Apollo)

Joe Turi

OF ALL THE RIDERS IN ALL THE WORLD who have show jumped internationally, Joe Turi must be the one with the most unlikely tale to tell of his rise to stardom. Born on 18 November 1956, Jozsef Turi had, as the saying goes, horses in his blood. He came from a nation of men for whom breeding, training, riding and driving horses was second nature. As a boy all his spare time was spent at the local riding stables, and the day he switched on the television and saw show jumping was the day he decided what he wanted to do with his life.

There was just one stumbling block: he was Hungarian. And show jumping in Hungary, as in so many other countries after the Second World War, had all but slid into oblivion – certainly at international level – following the disbanding of the cavalry. Whereas in the West the sport was quickly resurrected by civilians and tailored to meet the needs of a changing world, in Eastern Europe it did not merely mark time but went into regression in a totally different political and economic climate. With the exception of the much-depleted Moscow Games of 1980, which were boycotted by all the leading equestrian countries, the last time a Hungarian team had competed in the Nations Cup at the Olympics had been in 1928, and a Hungarian rider had not

Above: *From trick-rider to Olympic show jumper: Joe Turi riding Vital in the individual final at the 1988 Olympics*

Joe and Kruger, who has proved himself a top Nations Cup horse

won a show jumping medal since 1936.

For Joe, born in the town of Nagykoros, south of Budapest, the prospects of success looked bleak indeed. His love of horses caused him to fall out with his parents, who had no equestrian connections and were unable to understand their son's obsession. But his father, who wanted him to train as an electrician, finally capitulated. He found Joe a job at the renowned Bugac trick-riding school, where riding and caring for the herds of horses on the vast Hungarian plains came as second nature to the slightly built, athletic teenager. Unwittingly, his father had set in motion the train of events that was to lead his talented son to fame and fortune and, for many years, self-imposed exile.

In 1973, when he was seventeen, Joe travelled to England with the trick-riding group to perform at Wembley. A brief glimpse of the British horse scene was all that was needed to make him want to stay. As he was travelling back to the coast to go home, he decided – along with a friend – to jump from the lorry and seek political asylum. He spoke no English and knew only one Hungarian family, whom he had met briefly at Wembley. It was a question of living on his wits and going wherever fortune took him.

Things were certainly difficult to begin with. For the first couple of years he eked out an existence doing whatever jobs he could find. These included working at a riding school, for horse dealer Louis Soloman (who predicted that he would never make a show jumping rider!) and a spell with a Newmarket trainer. Then in 1975 he met Michael Bullman, himself a keen horseman, who combined show jumping up to Grade A level with working in his family shipping and ship-repairing business.

Michael, who at that time lived in Essex, had noticed Joe schooling a horse he had bought cheaply on the only bit of land he could find – a local roundabout. Joe had a job with the General Chip Company delivering shavings, and rode in his spare time, mostly late at night. Michael was so intrigued that he offered him some youngsters to ride, and so began a partnership that has become one of the most successful in the annals of British show jumping.

Still totally untutored when it came to jumping, Joe learned by absorbing all that Michael could teach him and by watching others. 'All you need,' he says, 'is a good horse, a little bit of talent, plenty of guts and determination. Then you learn by going to shows.' He makes it sound simple, but all those who have tried and failed know that it takes a special talent to reach the top of the international tree. Joe has that special talent, plus unlimited dedication, and Michael's eye for a horse has provided him with some very good equine partners indeed, notably Kruger and Vital.

Joe demonstrating the trick-riding skills he learned in his native Hungary

In 1986, not long after being granted British citizenship, Joe made his official debut for his adopted homeland at Falsterbo, in Sweden. Riding the Dutch warmblood stallion Vital (known at home as Herbie), he was a member of the team which won the Nations Cup. The former trick-rider's dream had come true. And there was more, much more, to follow.

Further successes abroad led to selection as non-travelling reserve for the 1987 European Championship team, and at the end of that year Joe signed his first sponsorship deal. He celebrated by winning the Volvo World Cup Qualifier at Olympia with Vital, beating among others the reigning European champion, Pierre Durand. In his first World Cup final in Gothenburg the following spring, Joe finished a very creditable ninth.

That summer Joe's other top ride, the Cornish-bred Kruger (otherwise known as George), really came into his own, proving himself a brilliant Nations Cup horse. He helped Britain to win in both Rome and Dublin, where he jumped a double clear. That clinched Joe's selection for the Seoul Olympics, and he was in the enviable position of being the only member of the British team with two horses at his disposal.

Contrary to the expectations of both owner and rider, it was the stallion, Vital, who better stood up to the long journey and change of climate, and who was duly put into the team. Vital went superbly in the first round of the Nations Cup, making just a single mistake, a feat that only one of his team-mates, David Broome's Countryman, was able to emulate. But, like so many of the horses that day, he tired in the second round and collected 16 faults. The British team finished out of the medals in sixth place, but Joe had acquitted himself honourably in his first major championship, alongside such seasoned internationals as Broome, Pyrah and Skelton.

In the individual final he was again superb in the first round, collecting a debatable 4 faults at the water (the splash could well have been caused by dirt kicked back as Vital landed) and a quarter of a time fault. Second time round he hit two fences, but at this level it was still good enough to put him in fourteenth place overall. Without the time fault, he would have been seventh. Not a bad effort for a man with only two years' experience at top international level.

The following year Joe contributed to no fewer than four Nations Cup successes: Aachen and Oberanven, where Kruger jumped double clears, and Dublin and Calgary, where Vital produced a clear round each time. But the highlight of his year – indeed, of his career – was his first championship medal: a team gold in the Europeans in Rotterdam where he and Kruger jumped clear in the first round of the Nations Cup, something which even

Joe on Mark Two

the mighty Milton failed to do. Even without counting Milton's score, the British team, comprising Joe, Nick Skelton and Michael Whitaker, had won the gold. It was a brilliant effort by any standards, and the more so since Kruger, whose health had been a bit suspect that summer, was later found to have a blood disorder which sidelined him for several months.

The day after the victory celebrations – it was Britain's third title in a row – Joe was the only member of the team to appear his usual bright, chatty self, ready to take on the next challenge. The reason? Unlike his team-mates, he is a teetotaller.

If Joe's rise to fame reads like a fairy tale, it should not be forgotten that it cost him dear in some ways. As a defector, it was many years before he was permitted to return to Hungary. He and his father never met again and although he was eventually reunited with his mother, she too died without seeing her son ride at the Olympics or stand on the victory podium at the European Championships. Nowadays his sole remaining relative is a half-brother.

Uprooting himself from home and family was the price he had to pay for the lifestyle he enjoys today, a lifestyle that must seem a

Joe and Vital coming out of the notoriously difficult Devil's Dyke at Hickstead in 1988, when they won the Derby Trial and were equal second in the Derby itself

Above left: *Joe receives a rosette from FEI President The Princess Royal at Hickstead*

million miles away from the plains of Hungary. Based at Michael Bullman's well-appointed yard at Wardington, in Oxfordshire, Joe rides valuable horses, wears the Union Jack on his saddle cloth, drives a smart car and can afford to take regular holidays in his native land. When he has the leisure he enjoys a game of tennis, but mostly it is still horses that dominate his life. Time was when he was invited to overseas shows only because people wanted to see his much-admired trick-riding displays. Now, he earns his invitations as one of the top half-dozen riders in Britain.

Joe – always cheerful and very popular

Career Highlights

1986   Falsterbo Nations Cup, winning team (Vital)
       Everest Double Glazing Championship, Hickstead
          (Vital)
       Eindhoven Jumping Derby (Vital)
1987   World Cup Qualifier, Olympia (Vital)
1988   Rome Nations Cup, winning team (Kruger)
       Dublin Nations Cup, winning team (Kruger)
1989   European Championships, team gold medal (Kruger)
       Hickstead Derby, second place (Kruger)
       Aachen Nations Cup, winning team (Kruger)
       Oberanven Nations Cup, winning team (Kruger)
       Dublin Nations Cup, winning team (Vital)
       Calgary Nations Cup, winning team (Vital)

David Broome

Above: *David Broome riding one of his great favourites, Sportsman, at Dublin*

Twenty-eight years after making his Olympic debut, David showed in Seoul that he had lost none of his artistry and enthusiasm. Conjuring a brilliant performance from the comparatively inexperienced Countryman, he finished only just out of the individual medals

Variously described as the greatest rider the world has seen, the finest ambassador of show jumping since the war, and a legend in his own lifetime, David Broome has played a starring role in British sport for three decades. The only rider to win three Men's European Championships (before the event was thrown open to both men and women in 1975), the only rider to win the historic King George V Gold Cup at the Royal International Horse Show five times, the only rider to take six National Championships, and the only male British rider to win a world title, he has more unique claims to fame than any other show jumper in the land.

Over a period of three decades, this affable, good-natured Welshman has been the best team member any chef d'équipe could wish for. He has a deep concern for the sport which has given him his livelihood, and in his capacity as president of the International Riders' Club he is a respected spokesman, not least in the riders' negotiations with the sport's governing body, the Fédération Equestre Internationale. For his services to show jumping he received an OBE in the 1970 New Year's Honours List. At the age of fifty he has lost little of his competitiveness (despite breaking his leg while out exercising early in 1990) and is still a formidable adversary on the international circuit.

David was born in Monmouthshire on 1 March 1940 and still lives at Mount Ballan Manor, Portskewett, where his family has farmed since the 1940s and where for many years they have run the well-known Wales and the West shows. He is married to Liz, sister of fellow show jumper Graham Fletcher, and they have three sons, James, Matthew and Richard, who all have ponies.

Steeped in horses from childhood, David was encouraged (though never forced) to ride and train ponies by his father, Fred – like his father before him an all-round horseman, with a particular interest in Welsh ponies and cobs. David was given Shetland ponies to ride at the age of two, and it was not long before he had graduated to Welsh Section As. However, his precocious equestrian career nearly ended when he was five and a newly broken pony he was riding gave him one fall too many. He decided to give up riding, and his father wisely did not try to dissuade him.

When he did, of his own volition, show an interest again, Fred bought him another pony, and after that there was no stopping him. He acquired the taste for jumping when he began hunting shortly afterwards, and it was not long before competitive show jumping became his chief recreation.

Although his mother was keen for all four children – David, his sisters Liz and Mary, and younger brother Frederick – to have a good education and not skip lessons simply to go to horse shows, by the time he was in his teens her elder son had already made up his mind that show jumping was going to be his life. Learning all he could from his father, whom he has always acknowledged as the architect of his success – the brains behind the operation – and by studying the riding of top internationals such as Pat Smythe and Colonel Sir Harry Llewellyn, both of whom lived nearby, David quickly progressed from top pony rider of Wales to national and international star. Allied to his remarkable natural talent for riding and jumping was, and still is, a perfect match temperament. Not one to show excesses of emotion, he takes both success and disappointment in his stride, imparting his calm outlook on life to the many horses he rides.

In 1959, at the age of only nineteen, he became leading money winner in Britain with his first top-class horse, Wildfire, bought by his canny father for less than £100. Then the following year David did what no British show-jumping rider had done before: he won an individual medal at the Olympic Games. Riding the ebullient Sunsalve, a horse that David recalls always went best when he thought he was running away with you, the twenty-year-old from Wales won the bronze medal, beaten only by the mighty d'Inzeo brothers, Raimondo and Piero. With typical thoroughness, Fred Broome, not wishing to risk Sunsalve becoming upset

Relaxing at home with Lannegan

by air travel, had himself driven the horse to those Rome Games, an arduous undertaking at that time. Showing amazing consistency, Sunsalve also put up the third-best performance in the separate Nations Cup, though sadly the British team as a whole was eliminated.

Sunsalve, on whom David won his first King George V Gold Cup not long before the Games and later, in 1961, the first of his Men's European Championships, was the horse of a lifetime. David's eyes still light up at the mention of his name and he remembers as if it were yesterday the 'feel' that this brave, brilliant horse gave him over certain fences. He is, incidentally, the only horse to have won both the King George V Gold Cup and the female riders' equivalent, the Queen Elizabeth II Cup, at the Royal International. Before David took over the ride, he had won the Queen's Cup in 1957 when ridden by his owner's daughter, Elizabeth Anderson.

Aboard the incomparable Sunsalve at the 1961 Royal International Horse Show, White City

At the three Olympics after Rome, David rode his brother-in-law Ted Edgar's horse Jacapo (Tokyo 1964), Mister Softee (Mexico 1968) and Manhattan (Munich 1972). In Tokyo the team finished fourth and David was down in twenty-first place, but team-mate Peter Robeson kept the flag flying by winning a jump-off for the individual bronze. Four years later in Mexico it was David's turn to jump off for third place, against three formidable adversaries: Frank Chapot (USA), Hans Günter Winkler (Federal Republic of Germany) and Jim Elder (Canada). All four went clear, but it was the big-hearted Mister Softee who scored the best time to give David a second bronze medal.

Two years later at La Baule David again demonstrated his superlative horsemanship by winning the Men's World Championship, in which the four finalists had to ride each other's horses. He recorded clear rounds with his own mount, Douglas Bunn's outstanding Beethoven, and with Graziano Mancinelli's Fidux and Harvey Smith's Mattie Brown. Only with Alwin Schockemöhle's Donald Rex did he have a fence down, but since his nearest rival, Mancinelli, could manage only two clears, David deservedly took the title with a clear margin.

At the Munich Olympics, Manhattan, a horse David described as having great ability but not much in the way of brains, finished only fourteenth in the individual; but he jumped well in the first round of the team event to finish on 4 faults, and Britain had a chance of the team bronze. Unfortunately, as he went into the arena for his second round, Manhattan had to pass the athletes gathering with their flags in readiness for the closing ceremony, and he became so fussed by all the noise that he collected 16 faults. Britain missed the bronze by one fence.

It was to be David's last Olympics for sixteen years. In 1973 he was deemed to be a professional, and not until 1987, when under a new ruling he successfully applied to be reclassified as a 'competitor', did he again become eligible for the Games. Since he was riding as well as ever, the selectors lost no time in shortlisting him for Seoul in 1988. He was duly chosen for the team and conjured a brilliant performance from the comparatively inexperienced young horse Countryman in the individual final to finish equal fourth – in spite of the fact that Countryman had pulled off a shoe during the first round and, as a result, become unbalanced towards the end of the course. For David to finish that close to a medal after thirty years in the sport was both frustrating but also calculated to fire him with enthusiasm to continue.

Throughout his jumping career David has had the valuable backing of his family – in particular his sister Mary, who for years was an indispensable 'backroom boy', especially when it came to schooling horses. He has been fortunate, too, in having both the

Douglas Bunn's Beethoven, the horse with whom David became World Champion in 1970

sponsorship support and friendship of Sir Phil Harris, who has provided him with some wonderful partners, among them the expensive grey ex-racehorse Philco, imported from the United States. It was on Philco that he helped Britain win a team gold in the 1978 World Championships, having won a team silver the previous year in the Europeans.

Mister Softee (winner of two European titles, in 1967 and 1969), Queensway Big Q (team European gold medallist in 1979), Mr Ross (world team bronze medallist in 1982 and European team silver medallist in 1983) and Sportsman (King George V Gold Cup winner in 1972 and National Champion in 1979) are just four of the many and varied horses that David has taken to the top. As he goes into the nineties with horses to ride of the calibre of Countryman and his stablemate Lannegan, it is unlikely that David will be thinking of hanging up his boots just yet.

Career Highlights

1960   Olympic Games, individual bronze medal (Sunsalve)
       Men's World Championship bronze medal (Sunsalve)
       King George V Gold Cup (Sunsalve)
1961   Men's European Championship, gold medal (Sunsalve)
       National Champion (Discutido)
1962   National Champion (Wildfire III/Grand Manan)
1966   King George V Gold Cup (Mister Softee)
1967   Men's European Championship, gold medal (Mister Softee)
       National Champion (Mister Softee)
1968   Olympic Games, individual bronze medal (Mister Softee)
1969   Men's European Championship, gold medal (Mister Softee)
1970   Men's World Championship, gold medal (Beethoven)
1972   King George V Gold Cup (Sportsman)
1973   National Champion (Sportsman)
1977   European Championships, team silver medal (Philco)
       King George V Gold Cup (Philco)
1978   World Championships, team gold medal (Philco)
1979   European Championships, team gold medal (Queensway Big Q)
       National Champion (Sportsman)
1981   King George V Gold Cup (Mr Ross)
1982   World Championships, team bronze medal (Mr Ross)
1983   European Championships, team silver medal (Mr Ross)
1986   National Champion (Phoenix Park)

Liz Edgar

F OR SOMEONE WHO DOES NOT much enjoy jumping under pressure, Liz Edgar has notched up a remarkable string of successes during her long career in the saddle. Five times the winner of the Queen Elizabeth II Cup at the Royal International, twice National Champion and the first woman to win the Aachen Grand Prix, one of the toughest events in the world, she has been one of Britain's top dozen riders for more than a decade. Ask any girl show jumper which senior rider she most admires and the answer is invariably 'Liz Edgar'. Her quiet, elegant style, wonderful eye for a stride and unfailing ability to get horses jumping in a beautifully balanced and rhythmic way are admired by everyone in the sport and have been an inspiration to many an aspiring young rider.

Liz was born on 28 May 1943, the second child of Millie and Fred Broome, and grew up at Mount Ballan Manor surrounded by ponies. Like her older brother David, she was taught to ride by her father and was soon competing successfully on ponies. Some she took over from David as he outgrew them, others were bought specially for her. Always they were acquired cheaply by her shrewd father.

Unlike her daughter Marie, Liz enjoyed school but, as with all

Above: *Liz Edgar's great favourite Forever enjoying some Polo mints at home*

Forever in action. This handsome Oldenburg gelding's many victories included the Aachen Grand Prix, and the Queen Elizabeth II Cup on three occasions

37

young riders, the time came when she had to choose between higher education and a life dedicated to horses, and in the end the latter prevailed. As a teenager working full-time for her father, she began to have considerable success with two mares – Bess, formerly ridden by David, and Ballan Excelsior. In 1960 she made her international debut with Ballan Excelsior at Amsterdam and was a member of the winning team in the Junior European Championships in Venice, where her partner was Gay Monty. She won the Young Riders' Championship of Great Britain at Hickstead two years running, in 1960 and 1961.

Invited to ride with the senior team in 1963, she made her Nations Cup debut in Ostend that August a winning one, and then jumped a double clear round in Rotterdam to help Britain score a second victory in a week. Her partner on both occasions was Bess.

The following year, on her birthday, Liz became engaged to Ted Edgar, whose reputation as a hell-raiser must have given Liz's parents more than a few sleepless nights. During the summer Liz continued her winning ways by taking the Ladies' National Championship on Bess and the National Championship on Ted's horse Jacapo, and it was with the latter that her brother David went to the Tokyo Olympics. She and Ted were married at the end of the year and moved into their new home, a bungalow called 'Ponderosa' at Ted's family farm, situated in the village of Leek Wootton in Warwickshire. Since then Ted's superlative eye for a horse has provided Liz, and more recently Marie, with a constant supply of talented jumpers.

For some years Ted continued to compete himself. One of his most famous successes was winning the 1969 King George V Gold Cup on the ex-American rodeo horse Uncle Max. But then, competing on a rodeo horse would probably seem like an everyday occurrence to someone who had, in 1963, ridden round the Hickstead Derby course one-handed after injuring his left arm a few days earlier. Douglas Bunn, the Master of Hickstead, had offered Ted a crate of champagne if he could complete the course despite having his left arm in a sling. In fact, with only 8 faults he not only won the champagne but also finished in the placings!

It was not long after Uncle Max won the King's Cup that David Kingsley of Everest Double Glazing came into the Edgars' lives. To begin with he arranged for the company to lease a couple of horses. Then in the early seventies came more substantial backing, and over the years the Edgar/Everest partnership blossomed into one of the most successful such enterprises in the sport.

A succession of good horses ridden by Liz and all carrying the Everest prefix have included Mayday, with whom she won the Ladies' National Championship at Royal Windsor in 1975; Wallaby, Queen Elizabeth II Cup and New York Grand Prix winner in 1977, and the Oldenburg gelding Forever, who was to become the best horse Liz has ridden.

Forever was foaled in Germany in 1972. Like another great show jumper, Sir Harry Llewellyn's Foxhunter, his birthday fell on 23 April (an auspicious day indeed, being both St George's day and Shakespeare's birthday). Ted bought him at the end of 1976 from the German dealer Axel Wockener. A grandson of that famous sire of jumpers, the thoroughbred Furioso, Forever had been operated on for a wind problem and when Liz first set eyes on him early in 1977 he was in such poor condition that she was far from impressed. Until, that is, she saw him jump.

In the Edgars' skilled hands, Forever gradually filled out his handsome, 17-hand frame, and was nursed by Liz through Newcomers, Foxhunter and Grade B. By the middle of 1979 he had made such tremendous strides that he was notching up victories at show after show, among them the Queen's Cup at the Royal

Liz on the Hanoverian Rapier, otherwise known as 'The Bull'

International. The following year he won the Grand Prix at Hickstead in May before going to Aachen. It was Liz's debut at the famous German show, a preparatory outing for the amateur riders whom the British selectors were hoping to send to the International Jumping Festival in Rotterdam (the 'alternative Olympics'). Forever showed his class by winning the Grand Prix, which had first been run in 1925 and which had never before been won by a woman.

Despite this tremendous achievement, Liz did not go to Rotterdam. She felt that Forever was not right, and he was later found to be suffering from a virus. It was to be twelve months before he hit international form again. He jumped a double clear round at the 1981 Aachen show to help Britain win the Nations Cup, and went on to win Liz her third Queen's Cup at the Royal International before being selected for the European Championships in Munich, where the British team finished fourth. His successes in 1982 included the Ladies' National Championship, the Queen's Cup yet again and the Lucerne Nations Cup.

Liz's partnership with Forever continued to flourish and included further Nations Cup successes, at Hickstead and Dublin in 1985. But in the summer of 1986 the Edgars received an offer for him which they could not refuse, and he was sold abroad. In 1988, at the age of sixteen, he acquitted himself most honourably at the Seoul Olympics where he looked after his Korean rider Shung-Hwan Kim in exemplary fashion, while Kim's equally inexperienced team-mates were getting into all sorts of difficulties on less talented schoolmasters.

Since the departure of Forever, Liz has enjoyed continued success with two horses owned by the Countess of Inchcape, the Hanoverian Everest Rapier and the British-bred Everest Asher. Rapier was runner-up in the Foxhunter Championship at Wembley in 1984. Liz has always blamed herself for giving him a bad ride in the last round, and says that if she had not 'messed him up' he would have won it. The following year she did win it, with Asher.

At home Rapier is jokingly known as 'The Bull', because when Ted first set eyes on him he took one look at his big white face and chestnut colouring and said, 'He looks just like a Hereford bull!' Whatever his looks, 'The Bull' is no mean performer. In 1986 he gave Liz a record fifth win in the Queen's Cup, equalling her brother David's tally in the King's Cup, and in Helsinki at the end of October 1987 Liz won the World Cup Qualifier with him, defeating a handful of top-class competitors in the jump-off, including her brother. It was the sort of situation in which Liz is at her best. Drawn first, she recorded a fast, accurate clear which made the others go flat out trying to catch her. She much prefers to

The British-bred Asher, with whom Liz won the Foxhunter Championship in 1985 after finishing runner-up the previous year with Rapier

go early in a jump-off and simply do her best rather than having the pressure of jumping last and knowing exactly what she has to beat.

Placing horses in the right competition at the right time is one of the many skills at which the Edgars excel. In 1988, twenty-four years after her victory with Jacapo, Liz took the National Championship for the second time, on this occasion with Rapier. After torrential rain the ground conditions at the Royal Show were appalling, and Liz attributed her success to the fact that Rapier was given a rest the day before the championship.

Such careful planning is typical of the entire Edgar operation, which is still based in Warwickshire at an ultra-modern yard and home called 'Rio Grande', built in the early eighties not far from their original home. Ted, with his flair for finding good horses and training both them and their riders, and Liz, with her love of bringing on young horses, have for more than two decades had a profound influence on British show jumping. It was under their tutelage that the talents of riders such as Nick Skelton, Lesley McNaught and Janet Hunter blossomed. With Emma-Jane Mac and young Marie continuing that tradition, and Liz still going on her quiet, winning way, the Edgar influence looks set to endure well into the nineties.

Career Highlights

1960   Junior European Championships, team gold medal (Gay
       Monty)
1964   National Champion (Jacapo)
       Ladies' National Champion (Bess)
1975   Ladies' National Champion (Mayday)
1977   Queen Elizabeth II Cup (Wallaby)
       New York Grand Prix (Wallaby)
1979   Queen Elizabeth II Cup (Forever)
1980   Aachen Grand Prix (Forever)
1981   Queen Elizabeth II Cup (Forever)
1982   Ladies' National Champion (Forever)
       Queen Elizabeth II Cup (Forever)
1986   Queen Elizabeth II Cup (Rapier)
1988   National Champion (Rapier)

Pierre Durand

WHATEVER HE ACHIEVES IN THE FUTURE, Frenchman Pierre Durand looks set to go down in show jumping history as the last true amateur to win an Olympic gold medal. In an age when the world's top riders have become, in all but name, professionals – certainly most work full-time with horses, whatever their financial status – Pierre has proved that it is possible to hold down a responsible job and still become a sporting star, always providing you have sufficient talent, dedication and the right horsepower.

Born near Bordeaux on 16 February 1955, Pierre had his first contact with horses through his father, Serge, an industrialist who together with a couple of friends developed an interest in hunting, bought some horses, and then was instrumental in setting up a riding centre for young people at St-Seurin-sur-l'Isle. It was there that Pierre learnt to ride – in fact he never studied anywhere else. For a short time he had tuition from visiting international three-day event rider Dominique Bontéjac, but mostly he has improved his style and technique simply by watching and talking to other top riders.

Thanks to his achievements, and the initiative and enthusiasm of the mayor of the town which actually owns the school, the latter

The spring-heeled little Jappeloup and Pierre Durand heading for Olympic gold in Seoul

has expanded quite a bit since then. Nowadays it evens boasts an indoor manège – appropriately named the 'Manège Pierre Durand'. But it still comes as a considerable surprise to find an Olympic champion based in one small corner of what is basically a modest rural riding stables.

Pierre enjoyed success at both national and international level as a junior before graduating in political science and pursuing a career as a bankruptcy official. Although he has always been devoted to his equestrian career, over the years his profession left him with only limited time for riding. His horses, always few in number, were and still are stabled at the St-Seurin Centre Equestre (he has never had his own yard at home), where he would go in the evenings to train them. Competing was, for the most part, restricted to weekends, with the result that he rode far fewer horses and had many less miles on the clock than his rivals on the senior circuit.

When he qualified for the change-horse final of the 1986 World Championships, the experts predicted that he would be the one of the four who would come away without a medal. And so it proved to be: he finished last, 22 faults behind bronze medallist Nick Skelton. Yet twelve months later he was champion of Europe, and a year after that Olympic champion. It was the stuff that film scripts are made of, and with his dark good looks, personable manner and keen intelligence, Pierre is well fitted to be a star. So too, of course, is his accomplice, the bouncy little Jappeloup, whose cat-like jump and sparkling personality have made him one of the most popular show jumpers of all time.

Jappeloup, who takes his name from the area where he was born, was foaled in 1975. By a trotter, Tyrol II, out of a thoroughbred mare Vénérable, he is technically a dark brown

43

Selle Français, though he looks black at first sight and is certainly not a typical stamp of Selle Français. Standing only a fraction over 15.2 hands, he has a natural tendency to be clumsy – he is adept at standing on people's feet – and is far from a comfortable ride, lacking the harmonious paces usually associated with the French riding horse.

When Pierre first had the chance to buy him as a three-year-old he turned him down because of his size. But fate was determined that the two should get together, and Pierre finally took him on in 1980. By 1982 the pair were champions of France. By no means the easiest of rides, Jappeloup has always been spooky and used to have a tendency to put in a lightning stop, dropping his ever loyal rider into the fence, slipping out of his bridle in the process, and galloping off round the arena. He did it during the second round of the Los Angeles Olympics and was eliminated for his pains.

Once they got their act together, however, the pair became one of the most feared combinations on the international circuit, even though Pierre, competing as he did far less than his rivals, at one time had a reputation for cracking under pressure. But he showed no signs of doing that at the 1987 European Championships when by holding off the challenge of John Whitaker and Milton he became the first Frenchman to take the individual title; and his performance in the Olympic Games the following year was one of the most memorable in jumping history. Taking a calculated gamble by going slowly and incurring a total 1.50 time faults, Pierre put Jappeloup right at every fence. They were the only combination not to incur jumping faults in the two rounds – what better way to win a gold medal? Pierre's proud father was there to see his son's magnificent achievement. But his mother, Arlette, who had been to a show many years earlier only to see him fall, is too panic-stricken ever to watch – even on television!

Later that year Pierre, who had been contemplating retiring after Seoul, decided instead to give up his work in the law and concentrate full-time on jumping, under the management of the International Management Group, whose other sporting clients include Pierre's compatriot, skier Jean-Claude Killy. As a back-up to Jappeloup he bought, at the beginning of 1989, the Selle Français mare Narcotique, who is by the noted French jumping stallion Impédoumi. The 1992 Olympics are his long-term objective.

Pierre still lives in the delightful vine-growing region of Bordeaux, some fifteen minutes' drive from his stables. He and his wife Nadia, also an accomplished rider, have a young daughter, Lisa. Hardly surprisingly, she is already keen on ponies. Meanwhile, the other important member of the family, Jappeloup, still occupies his box at the modest St-Seurin Equestrian Centre.

Studying the course is a serious business

Nowadays visiting dignitaries to the town find that an expedition to see the little wonder horse tends to take precedence over the more traditional trip to the region's delightful châteaux. And just down the road they will find that the local baker is doing a roaring trade in his special Jappeloup cake – a delicious concoction of chocolate, coffee, praline and macaroons devised specially in the little horse's honour.

Jappeloup proved that lack of inches is no handicap when winning his first major title, the European Championship of 1987

Career Highlights

1982   National Champion (Jappeloup)
1983   Mediterranean Games, team silver medal (Jappeloup)
1985   World Cup, third place (Jappeloup)
1986   World Championships, team bronze medal and fourth place individually (Jappeloup)
        National Champion (Jappeloup)
1987   European Championships, individual gold and team silver medals (Jappeloup)
1988   Olympic Games, individual gold and team bronze medals (Jappeloup)
        World Cup, second place (Jappeloup)
1989   European Championships, team silver medal (Jappeloup)
1990   World Cup, second place (Jappeloup)

Ian Millar

RARELY SEEN AT EUROPEAN SHOWS because of the huge distances they have to travel, Canadian riders have a habit of taking the rest of the show jumping world unawares when they turn out in force at major championships. In recent years, none has been more successful than Ian Millar, whose partnership with the aptly named Big Ben has made him one of the most feared adversaries on the international scene.

A regular member of the Canadian team for nigh on twenty years, 'Big Ian' – at 6ft 2in he is one of the tallest riders in the world – made his Olympic debut in Munich in 1972 when the team, including Jim Elder, Jim Day and Terrance Millar (no relation) finished sixth. Four years later in Montreal the team, this time comprising Ian, Elder, Day and Michel Vaillancourt, who went on to win the individual silver, were placed fifth, only 1.50 faults behind the bronze medal-winning Belgians. And four years after that, at the International Jumping Festival in Rotterdam, the Canadians, with Mark Laskin replacing Jim Day, captured the gold in a hotly contested team event.

Ian's partner that day was the ten-year-old thoroughbred gelding Brother Sam, with whom he had finished ninth individually in the 1978 World Championships in Aachen (the team was fourth)

Ian Millar with the gentle giant Big Ben, twice a winner of the World Cup and the first horse to win all three legs of the final

and twelve months later had won the individual bronze medal and a team silver in the Pan American Games, held in Puerto Rico. In Rotterdam, where the courses were huge, Brother Sam collected only 4.50 faults in the two rounds, which was the ninth-best score of the entire thirteen-nation championship.

It was in 1983 that Big Ben came into Ian's life. Bred in Belgium in 1976, Ben (formerly called Winston) is a handsome chestnut warmblood gelding by the French stallion Etretat. Standing 17.3 hands and built in proportion, he has a charisma that makes even the most jaundiced audience sit up and take notice. He was purchased in Holland and is now owned by a syndicate called Canadian Show Jumpers Unlimited Inc. By the late eighties he had become, together with Jappeloup and Milton, one of the three most outstanding horses in the world, and is fortunate in having found the ideal partner in Ian Millar.

Ian, born on 6 January 1947, has not, like so many British riders, devoted his entire life to horses. Although he was keen on riding and other sports as a child in Edmonton, he went on to study business administration and has had careers as a stockbroker, a radio broadcaster and a hotel and restaurant owner/operator. Today he lives with his wife Lynn and their children Jonathan and Amy on a farm near Perth in Ontario, where horses are currently very much a full-time occupation.

Personable, intelligent and articulate, Ian is a tremendous ambassador for show jumping. He learned at an early age to be a good loser as well as a good winner, and however much he feels the pressure of competing with a horse as famous as Big Ben, he gives precious little hint of it in his genial demeanour. Ian's riding of Big Ben is a marvel to watch, for despite the horse's size and his gigantic, ground-devouring stride, Ian makes him look as neat and handy as a pony in a jump-off against the clock.

Ian rode Big Ben at the 1984 Los Angeles Games where the Canadian team was beaten for the bronze by a mere three-quarters of a fault. In the individual Ian tied for fourteenth place (with John Whitaker and Ryan's Son, Pierre Durand and Jappeloup, and the Mexican Gerardo Tazzer Valencia on Magod). Later in the year the pair were in the winning Nations Cup team in New York.

But it is perhaps in the World Cup more than anywhere else that Ian has reigned supreme. His domination of the Canadian League, first run in 1983–84, has been very nearly complete. Only in 1988–89 (when there was no pressure to qualify because the holder is automatically guaranteed a place in the next final) did he not top the points ratings, and even then he finished a good third behind Mario Deslauriers and Lisa Carlsen.

Ian made his World Cup final debut in Baltimore in 1980, when

The Canadians swept to victory in the 1980 Rotterdam International Show Jumping Festival, staged for the countries which did not go to the Moscow Olympics. Ian is seen riding Brother Sam

he finished fourteenth on Bandit. He did not contest the final
again until Gothenburg in 1984 when he rode Wotan, another Belgian-bred horse, into eighteenth place. But when Big Ben made
his first appearance, in Berlin in 1985, Ian was immediately
among the top ten, finishing eighth behind Conrad Homfeld of the
United States.

The following year, back in Gothenburg, Ian and Ben were
runners-up to Leslie Burr-Lenehan of the United States and
McLain, and it began to look only a matter of time before they
would give Canada her second Cup victory (Mario Deslauriers
had won the trophy in 1984 with Aramis). At the Paris final in
1987 Ian and Ben tied for fifth place with John Whitaker and Milton. That August they took double gold in the Pan American
Games in Indianapolis, where they finished more than a fence in
hand over their nearest rival in the individual championship. In
April 1988, before the cheering 12,000-strong Gothenburg crowd,
they duly scored a brilliant World Cup victory over Durand and
Jappeloup, the pair who were to go on to become Olympic champions later in the year. Ian won the first leg, was equal fourth in
the second and equal third in the last.

Sadly, Ian's hopes of an Olympic medal in Seoul did not come
to fruition. The Canadians have twice in recent years lost a minor
medal by the narrowest of margins and Ian must have felt that,
with a partner such as Big Ben, his turn had come for either a team
or an individual medal – perhaps both.

Whether it was that energy-sapping World Cup victory, the extensive Canadian qualifying system for the Games, or simply the
long journey to Korea that caused Big Ben to be somewhat below
his brilliant best in Seoul, we shall never know. Ian, with his
typically intellectual approach, has tried to analyse the problem,
but without success. Although Ben did jump a clear second round
in the Nations Cup, which helped the Canadian team to finish a
very close fourth behind the medal-winning nations, Ian found in
the individual final, for which he started one of the favourites, that
he had simply 'run out of horse'. Ben began promisingly, with just
three-quarters of a time fault in the first round, but he looked a
tired horse in the second half, hit three fences and dropped to
fifteenth place overall.

However, the following spring in Tampa he was to write himself into the record books in no uncertain terms. Although one
rider – Conrad Homfeld – had previously won the World Cup
final twice, no one had done so two years running, or on the same
horse. The apparent effortlessness with which Ian and Big Ben
made history was breathtaking. They won the first leg, the speed
class, with almost indecent ease. They won the second, over one
round with two jump-offs. They won the third, over two rounds,

Ian, with his chef d'équipe *Tom Gayford, at the World Cup final, Tampa, in 1989*

with the only double clear (Milton was also clear but collected a quarter time fault). Thus Ben became the first horse to win all three legs and the first to win two finals, while Ian became the first rider to win consecutive finals and on the same horse. In doing so he had shown his genius by coping successfully with the many and varied problems set by that incomparable designer of courses, Bertalan de Nemethy. Big Ben was unfortunately prevented from going for a third World Cup victory in 1990. An operation for colic kept him out of action for several months.

Ian's considerable contribution to equestrian sport – apart from his many individual triumphs he has represented his country in more than fifty Nations Cups – has not gone unacknowledged. In 1986, the year in which he became the first Canadian to be ranked number one jumping rider in North America, he was awarded the Order of Canada for his outstanding representation of Canada in international sport and for the help that he gives to young riders.

Career Highlights

1979 Pan American Games, team silver and individual bronze medal (Brother Sam)
1980 International Show Jumping Festival, Rotterdam, team gold medal (Brother Sam)
1983 Pan American Games, team silver medal (Foresight)
National Champion
1984 World Cup Canadian League, winner
1985 World Cup Canadian League, winner
1986 World Cup, second place (Big Ben)
World Cup Canadian League, winner
National Champion
1987 Pan American Games, individual and team gold medals (Big Ben)
World Cup Canadian League, winner
1988 World Cup, winner (Big Ben)
World Cup Canadian League, winner
1989 World Cup, winner (Big Ben)
1990 World Cup Canadian League, winner

Franke Sloothaak

FRANKE SLOOTHAAK IS ONE OF A GROWING number of European riders who have switched nationality to further their riding careers. He was born in Holland on 2 February 1958 and his family home was at Rotsterhaule, some thirty kilometres south of Leeuwarden. While his brother followed their father into the building trade, Franke was more interested in the local Pony Club. He was never able to have ponies of his own at home, but by the time he was in his teens he was showing so much riding ability that people were asking him to compete with their horses, and he twice won team silver medals for his native land in the Junior European Championships: in Cork in 1972 at the age of only four-teen, and in Lucerne two years later. In Brussels in 1976 he was equal second in the individual championship.

All three medals were achieved on different horses, proving that one thing at which he did become adept at a very early stage was adapting to new equine partners each season. Most leading show jumpers, even juniors, enjoy fairly prolonged periods with their top horses, establishing long-term partnerships with them, to the benefit of both parties. But when you ride solely for other people, horses tend to come and go, to change riders, to be sold on, and it is Franke's adaptability and versatility, nurtured in those early

Above: Dutch-born Franke Sloothaak, who has spent most of his international career riding for the Federal Republic of Germany

Franke and Walzerkönig at the Seoul Olympics, where they helped Germany win a team gold medal

This book was written and passed for press before Paul Schockemöhle announced his withdrawal from the breeding and production of show jumpers following accusations, made in July 1990, of cruelty in training. It was therefore not possible to update the chapter referring to Franke Sloothaak, who up until that time rode for the Schockemöhle stable.

years, that make him such a valuable asset to any owner.

It was in 1975 that his future really began to be shaped. His horsemanship caught the eye of the German ace Alwin Schockemöhle, who recognised the young Franke's talent and took him under his wing. Alwin, who had previously ridden his father's racehorses and competed as a three-day eventer before turning to show jumping, was one of the most successful riders of the sixties and seventies, a regular member of the frequently unassailable West German team and European Champion in 1975. He crowned his career by winning the individual gold medal at the 1976 Olympics in Montreal. Riding Warwick Rex he jumped a double clear round, becoming the first and as yet the only rider to win the gold outright with a zero score and no jump-off.

But by this time the thirty-nine-year-old German ace knew that his career as an international rider was coming to an end. Chronic back trouble finally decided him to hang up his boots at the end of that Olympic year. And it was to his protégé, Franke Sloothaak, that he entrusted in due course the ride on his horses, among them the brilliant grey Rex the Robber, who in 1975 had helped Alwin sweep the board at Britain's CSIO, including a victory in the King George V Gold Cup.

Under Alwin's expert tutelage Franke's natural talents blossomed. For eight years Alwin provided him with a constant supply of good horses and Franke, having found the ideal base from which to operate, and receiving no invitations to ride with the Dutch team, eventually took German citizenship so that he could ride officially for his adopted country.

In 1980 he had a marvellous run of success in the World Cup qualifying competitions, winning in the spring on Rex the Robber in Dortmund, on the ex-Johan Heins horse Argonaut in Amsterdam in the autumn, and finishing runner-up, also with Argonaut, in Berlin shortly afterwards. In the 1981 final, held in Birmingham, he won the first leg and finished eleventh overall. He became National Champion of Germany with Argonaut in 1981, after finishing runner-up the previous year. His record in that event has been remarkable: second in 1984 and third in both 1985 and 1988, while in 1989 he recaptured the title. Also in 1981 he made his senior Nations Cup debut, being a member of the winning German team in both Liège and Dublin.

He first represented the Federal Republic in a Championship team in the Los Angeles Olympics of 1984 where he won a bronze medal and finished equal eleventh individually on Farmer, owned by Paul Schockemöhle, for whom he had started riding that year. With Alwin devoting himself more and more to training trotters, it was a natural step for Franke to move over to Alwin's brother Paul. He did not have far to move, since the brothers' yards are

Franke making history in Seoul, where he became only the second rider to win an Olympic team gold medal without jumping both rounds in the Nations Cup

within spitting distance of each other at Mühlen, where Franke still lives with his wife and two children.

Paul, youngest of the three Schockemöhle brothers, had come into show jumping relatively late in life, having first set himself up in business as a chicken farmer. He did not begin competing seriously until the late sixties. By the mid eighties he had established the most extensive private jumper breeding enterprise in the world, and with so many top-class horses on hand he had no difficulty in attracting talented riders like Franke to be his stable jockeys.

Paul once said that there was no horse in his establishment, with the exception of his irreplaceable Deister, which was not for sale. And that represents the only disadvantage of being attached to a professional dealing yard – a rider can, virtually overnight, see a brilliant horse sold from under him. But for someone without horses of his own it is a price worth paying for the security of knowing that there will always be other good ones coming along, and Franke has not exactly been strapped for equine talent since throwing in his lot with Paul. Because he is blessed with the temperament and the horsemanship to switch successfully from horse to horse as the occasion demands, he has been a highly successful performer for the Schockemöhle stable.

Franke and the big winner Argonaut

Farmer is a good example of a horse who has changed ownership not just once but on several occasions, and in quick succession. Indeed, at one time this useful Holsteiner seemed to be jet-setting back and forth across the Atlantic like a high-powered city executive. He has been ridden during his career by several Americans and at least one Canadian, usually returning between times to Paul's yard when Franke would again take up partnership with him.

Since riding Farmer at the Los Angeles Games, Franke has been a regular member of the German European Championship team, winning a bronze with Walido in 1985 and finishing fifth individually at Rotterdam in 1989 behind John Whitaker. His ride on that occasion was the exceptionally talented Hannoverian gelding Walzerkönig, the horse with whom he achieved the highlight of his career in 1988, a team gold medal at the Seoul Olympics. Walzerkönig had demonstrated his remarkable spring when as an eight-year-old he had cleared 7ft 2½in (2.20m) and then had a good stab at jumping 7ft 6½in (2.30m) in the 1987 Rome Puissance when partnered by his previous rider, Bernhard Kamps.

Of the sixty-four starters in the Nations Cup in Seoul, just four riders jumped a clear round without time faults. Franke, anchorman of the German squad, was one of them, the only person besides Switzerland's Markus Fuchs to be clear in the first round. By the time each country's third rider had gone a second time, the

Germans already had the gold in the bag, so Franke was able to save Walzerkönig for the individual. He thus became only the second rider in Olympic history to win a team gold without having jumped two rounds (Melanie Smith was the first, in Los Angeles). Unfortunately, in the individual final Walzerkönig did not reproduce that blistering form and Franke was one of seven riders to tie for seventh place on 12 faults.

Amiable, always approachable, Franke is a popular ambassador for show jumping wherever he goes. His relaxed yet dashing style of riding inspires horses to go well for him. He is also one of the most deadly of adversaries. Always a welcome visitor to Britain, he has a habit of snatching the biggest prizes from the home contingent. In 1988 alone he left the British Olympic short-listed riders trailing in his wake in the £18,000 Dubai Cup at Hickstead, and then returned later in the year to rub salt into the wound by collecting the Grands Prix at both Wembley and Olympia. Twelve months later he retained the big prize at Wembley, even though his top horse, Walzerkönig, was on the injured list – proving, if any proof were needed, that whenever there is a Sloothaak/Schockemöhle horse to jump, no one dare afford to rest on their laurels.

Career Highlights

1972 Junior European Championships, team silver medal
      (Sarno)
1974 Junior European Championships, team silver medal
      (Polo Marco)
1976 Junior European Championships, individual silver medal
      (San Angelo)
1981 National Champion
1984 Olympic Games, team bronze medal (Farmer)
1985 European Championships, team bronze medal (Walido)
1988 Olympic Games, team gold medal (Walzerkönig)
1989 National Champion
1990 World Cup, third place (Walzerkönig)

Thomas Frühmann

A COUPLE OF DAYS AFTER WINNING the 1989 Olympia World
Cup Qualifier, Thomas Frühmann, in common with other
continental visitors to London's pre-Christmas show, was to be
seen hastening home in readiness for the next important event.
Nothing unusual in that, one might think. Except that *his* subsequent destination was not an international showground but a
trotting racetrack.

Whenever his hectic jumping schedule permits, the genial
Austrian likes nothing better than to replace his hunting cap, red
coat and breeches with a crash hat, goggles and slacks, climb into
one of those frail-looking bike-wheel sulkies and whiz round a
raceway at thirty miles an hour. Indeed, at the time of writing he
needed only another dozen winners to qualify for a professional
driver's licence.

For Thomas, a native of Vienna, life without horses would be
unthinkable. But, realist that he is, he appreciates just how precarious that top-of-the-tree position in the world of show jumping,
which he achieved during the eighties, can be. And he has no intention of being left stranded should his current supply of good
horses suddenly dry up. When the time comes to give up riding
jumpers, he plans to switch to trotters. He sees it as an insurance

*Thomas Frühmann and the brilliant
Hanoverian stallion Grandeur*

policy; and a most enjoyable one at that.

Born on 23 January 1951 into a totally unhorsey family, Thomas was eight when he began attending a riding school in Vienna. By the time he was twelve he was competing with some success in jumping classes. Whatever their feelings on the matter, it soon became clear to his mother and father (the latter is a psychiatrist) that a conventional profession was not for their son. It was not so much that he was bad at school but the fact that he attended as little as possible that persuaded his parents to allow him to try to make a career for himself with horses.

Fortunately, he obtained the sort of grounding that would stand anyone with talent in good stead for the rest of their life. He was seventeen when he went to Munich to study with Ottokar Pohlmann, the former three-day event rider turned trainer who had won a team gold medal in the 1959 European Championships at Harewood in Yorkshire. Employed along the same sort of lines as a working pupil in a British riding establishment, Thomas learned all aspects of horsemanship and at the end of his three years' training graduated with the top German qualification.

Returning home to Austria at the age of twenty-one, he made his way for a number of years by teaching and competing with other people's horses. Then he acquired the former Fritz Ligges horse Donau, who gave him his first taste of success at international Grand Prix level. That, however, was away from home. Austria itself has so little top-level show jumping that it is simply not a suitable base for an ambitious rider, and having taken the measure of the national circuit, Thomas realised that if he wanted to make real headway on the international scene he would have to

A youthful Thomas on his first show jumper, the 14.2 hands pony Taurus. Taurus's owner, Mr Furth, was the first person to import jumping ponies into Austria

find himself an establishment elsewhere.

His decision to move back to Germany was a propitious one. He had not been there long when a chance encounter at a show brought him the security every rider dreams of: the job of stable jockey to a wealthy owner, in this case the head of the C & A stores. That was in 1980, and with a string of good horses at his disposal, including the big winners Bandit and Arizona, he soon began to make a name for himself on the European circuit. Yet such is the precarious nature of the show jumping game that only three years later this enviable arrangement came, abruptly, to an end. His sponsor, who had become a close friend, suddenly died. The end of a friendship. No more backing. No string of horses. Thomas was on his own again.

It could so easily have been the end of a promising career. But as luck would have it, there was in his late sponsor's yard a horse belonging to the former Olympic champion Alwin Schockemöhle. Since he retired from show jumping Alwin's chief occupation has been centred around trotters, but he has never totally relinquished his interest in jumpers. The ex-champion and the budding one got together, had a talk and the upshot of it was that Thomas moved to Alwin's yard at Mühlen. He has been there ever since. He and Alwin have developed a successful business partnership, operating on a fifty-fifty basis, with Alwin concentrating on the trotters and Thomas on the jumpers.

In recent years, with the exception of Hugo Simon, no one has done as much as Thomas to keep the Austrian show jumping flag flying. He made his Olympic debut on a horse called Star Favorit at Montreal in 1976, and although the team did not go well enough to compete in the second round of the Nations Cup, it was a significant occasion for the Austrians, who were mustering a full Olympic jumping team for the first time in twenty years.

Four years later, at the International Show Jumping Festival in Rotterdam, Thomas and Donau won a bronze medal in the hotly contested team championship. Thomas was one of only three riders to jump a double clear round. Indeed, if his compatriot Hugo Simon and the mighty Gladstone had shown the form which was to win them the individual gold two days later, Austria would have defeated Canada for the team gold.

Thomas, who became Austrian National Champion in 1987, did not contest the 1984 or 1988 Games and is not a great fan of major championships in general. He believes that they take too much out of a horse and that a rider is better employed competing at three or four ordinary international shows instead. Proving his point, during the eighties he twice finished runner-up (1981 and 1989) and was twice third (1982 and 1987) in the World Cup European League, which is a series of conventional Grand Prix-type competitions. But in the World Cup final itself, run in three strenuous legs over several days, his highest placing was fifteenth (1980). He has nevertheless been a regular competitor in the European Championships since 1977. At St Gallen in 1987 he finished just out of the individual medals, in fourth place, on the German-bred Porter, who was subsequently sold to Switzerland. Recently his biggest winner has been the brilliant Hanoverian stallion Grandeur, who in the three seasons 1987 to 1989 was victorious in no fewer than five World Cup preliminary rounds: the one at Olympia mentioned above, 's-Hertogenbosch, Bordeaux, Paris and Gothenburg.

Despite his size – he is over six feet tall and weighs in at around fourteen stone ('depending on the beer'!) – Thomas rides with

The big winner Porter, a horse who was subsequently sold to Switzerland

great dash and lightness, gifts which probably have something to do with the fact that, like most Austrians, he is a keen skier. He and his wife, Heidelinde, who is not a rider herself, live close to Alwin Schockemöhle's Mühlen stables, but three or four times a year they go to their other home in an Austrian ski resort for a break from the equestrian world.

Apart from skiing, Thomas's greatest interest lies in racing – not just the trotters which he drives for Alwin, but also flat racing. He talks enthusiastically of a two-year-old he had in training in Vienna in 1989, whose narrow defeat by a horse from the all-conquering Maktoum stable on his debut in Italy, and subsequent victory in his second race, evidently gave Thomas as big a kick as winning a major jumping class with Grandeur.

Thumbs up after winning the car in the Volvo World Cup Qualifier at Olympia, 1989

Career Highlights

1980   International Show Jumping Festival, Rotterdam, team
          bronze medal (Donau)
1981   World Cup European League, second place
1982   World Cup European League, third place
1983   World Cup Preliminary Competition, Bordeaux
          (Arizona)
1987   World Cup European League, third place
          World Cup Preliminary Competition, 's-Hertogenbosch
          (Grandeur)
          World Cup Preliminary Competition, Bordeaux
          (Grandeur)
          European Championships, fourth place individually
          (Porter)
          National Champion
1989   World Cup European League, second place
          World Cup Preliminary Competition, Paris (Grandeur)
          World Cup Preliminary Competition, Gothenburg
          (Grandeur)
          World Cup Preliminary Competition, Olympia
          (Grandeur)

Malcolm Pyrah

S AY THE NAME MALCOLM PYRAH and most show-jumping en-
thusiasts will automatically think of one particular horse, the
chestnut gelding with the memorable, if tongue-twisting name
Towerlands Anglezarke. But Yorkshire-born Malcolm, a top
international for nearly two decades, has never been a one-horse
rider. His achievements during the seventies with horses such as
Arksey, Law Court and the former show hack Lucky Strike testify
to that.

It was, however, his (and Britain's) good fortune that he should
have been paired with Anglezarke in 1980. They formed a
partnership that became a mainstay of the British team for most of
the decade. Apart from a tendency to put a foot or two in the water
(the reason why Malcolm preferred not to ride him at Hickstead,
with its big open water jump), Anglezarke was the perfect international jumper. He had been produced as a novice by Adrian

*Towerlands Anglezarke, the horse
with whom Malcolm Pyrah achieved
countless successes during the eighties*

64

Marsh and went to Malcolm's yard in 1980 from Trevor Banks. In their first major championship together, the 1981 World Cup final, the pair finished a promising eighth, and later that year Malcolm won the individual silver medal with him in the European Championships. Thereafter they became regular British team members, contributing to many Nations Cup successes and winning a team silver and two team golds in subsequent European Championships.

In the 1982 World Championships Malcolm qualified for the change-horse final and demonstrated his fine horsemanship by coping well, despite his own slight build, with the enormous German horse Fire. The final resulted in a runaway victory for Fire's young rider Norbert Koof, but in the jump-off for the lesser medals Malcolm effectively outrode Frenchman Michel Robert for the silver.

Malcolm was born on 26 August 1941, and although he competed at local shows on ponies as a boy, he made a late start as a senior show jumper. After leaving grammar school he worked in local government until he was going on twenty-three, continuing to ride in his spare time. By then he had started to build up a dry-cleaning business – today he is a director of a firm with eight shops – but it was a career with horses that he really wanted. He went to work for well-known owner Trevor Banks and subsequently for John Massarella, and for some ten years he rode their horses and gained experience on the national circuit.

In 1972 he married fellow rider Judy Boulter, winner of many good classes with her mare Fanny Hill, and the following year the couple set up their own yard in Nottinghamshire. It was to prove an ideal partnership, for Judy's expertise in schooling horses and producing them in tip-top condition has been a valuable asset to Malcolm throughout his international career. Anglezarke was the shining proof, if any were needed, of the Pyrahs' horse management skills; always produced in peak condition when it mattered most, even when he was well into his teens, he was a credit to them both.

A perfect example of this was when, as a sixteen-year-old, he ran off with the King George V Gold Cup and the Grand Prix at the 1987 Royal International Horse Show. He was the first horse in more than twenty years to win the King's Cup a second time, and no one was more thrilled than his charming and devoted owner, Mrs Edna Hunnable, whose infectious enthusiasm delighted so many people on the show circuit. Contrary to his usual practice, the shrewd Malcolm then decided to take Anglezarke to Hickstead for the Dubai Cup. Anglezarke cleared the big water jump as if he had been doing it all his life, and picked up the £17,500 first prize in breathtaking style.

Above: *A study in concentration and determination. Malcolm makes a dash for the car during a ride and drive competition at the Royal International Horse Show. He won the class*

Malcolm and Law Court, World Championship team gold medallists in 1978

Although Malcolm became a regular Nations Cup rider as long ago as 1973, he was unfortunately lost to the British Olympic team early on in his international career, being one of the first to be classified as a professional during the seventies – ironic, considering that he really did have a legitimate business outside the horse world. Consequently he could not partner Law Court, his top jumper at that time, in the 1976 Games and had to give the ride to amateur Peter Robeson, who finished in fourteenth place individually.

There was some consolation two years later when Malcolm and Law Court were selected for the first running of the World Team Championship at Aachen, where they helped secure the gold medal. Malcolm, whose record in the World Championships over the years demonstrates just what a loss he was to the Olympic team, went on to win a team bronze in 1982 and a silver in 1986. He contributed a clear round in the Nations Cup on each occasion with Anglezarke.

By the time of the 1988 Olympics, Malcolm had successfully applied to be reinstated as a 'competitor' rather than a professional, and he duly took his place with the now seventeen-year-old Anglezarke in the team for Seoul. Sadly, the Games had come just a little too late for the old horse and he seemed not to enjoy jumping on the deep sand surface in the team contest, in which he hit two fences in each round. Malcolm, not wanting him to end his career on a sour note, opted not to start in the individual final even though he was qualified to do so. He gave his place to Joe Turi and, having taken a look at the big first-round course for the final, said he was relieved he had.

After Anglezarke retired from jumping at the end of 1988, the Pyrahs kept him on for Judy to hunt. Malcolm, meanwhile, has continued competing, though on a reduced scale, with Towerlands Diamond Seeker, the young French-bred It's Me, and Lucky Me, who finished fourth in the 1989 Foxhunter Championship at Wembley.

Although he is in his fiftieth year, Malcolm has lost none of the skills that have taken him to so many international successes: a quick brain, a marvellous eye for a stride, determination, guts and an indomitable will to win. He still lives in Nottinghamshire – he, Judy and their daughter are based at Granby. He enjoys training both horses and riders and has been heard to good effect commentating on satellite television, but as long as he is fit and continues to derive satisfaction from it, he intends to go on competing.

Anglezarke at the Seoul Olympics, his last championship event before he was retired to the hunting field

Career Highlights

1978 World Championships, team gold medal (Law Court)
1979 European Championships, team gold medal (Law Court)
1981 European Championships, individual silver medal (Anglezarke)
1982 World Championships, individual silver and team bronze medals (Anglezarke)
1983 European Championships, team silver medal (Anglezarke)
1985 European Championships, team gold medal (Anglezarke)
    King George V Gold Cup (Anglezarke)
1986 World Championships, team silver medal (Anglezarke)
1987 European Championships, team gold medal (Anglezarke)
    King George V Gold Cup (Anglezarke)

The Americans

I T IS A CURIOUS PHENOMENON of recent years that while Europe
can scarcely muster half a dozen top women show jumpers, the
United States has produced an endless stream of talented eques-
triennes who give no quarter in the world's arenas. Katie
Monahan-Prudent, Leslie Burr-Lenehan, Anne Kursinski, Katharine Burdsall, Lisa Tarnopol, Deborah Dolan, Joan Scharffenberger, Melanie Smith, Terry Rudd, Lisa Jacquin – the list goes
on and on, and each and every one is championship material. The
Americans can, and do, make up entire Nations Cup teams of
female riders and go out there and win.

Indeed, at the Washington show in 1986 Anne Kursinski,
Katharine Burdsall, Lisa Tarnopol and Katie Monahan created
show jumping history by becoming the first all-female team to win
a Nations Cup since the first such contest in 1909. To prove it was
no fluke, twelve months later at Hickstead, while their team
leader George Morris was in hospital nursing a broken neck after
a horrific fall at one of Hickstead's permanent hedges, Joan
Scharffenberger and Deborah Dolan joined up with Anne and
Katie to lick the best teams from Europe. Three American girls
have won the fiercely contested World Cup final, and the United
States teams at the last two Olympics have been fifty per cent
female.

Katie Monahan-Prudent riding Nordic. Like so many top United States riders, Katie benefited from training with George Morris

Every one of them is a star in her own right, and no one has been more successful in the long term than **Katie Monahan-Prudent**. Born in the decidedly unequestrian setting of a Chicago suburb on 15 March 1954, Katie says she has been interested in horses ever since she learned to talk. Encouraged by her father she soon began to make an impression in equitation classes, and when she was in her teens (by which time the family had moved to Michigan) she got her first real break when she met up with USET member Chrystine Jones, whose advice and tutelage were to prove invaluable.

It was Sallie Sexton, the well-known judge whose horses she was riding, who first arranged for Katie to travel east to compete and who arranged for her to have a lesson with George Morris. Morris, who rode in the Olympics as long ago as 1960, was the single most powerful influence on the young Katie's career – just as he has been on the careers of so many other young riders. A brilliant horseman and a dedicated and gifted teacher, he more than anyone helped to mould Katie into the top international rider she is today, giving her in those early days a wide selection of horses to ride and reserving one in particular, the thoroughbred The Jones Boy, for her to compete on internationally.

It was with The Jones Boy that Katie so nearly won the first running of the World Cup final in Gothenburg in 1979. That was the one and only year in which the final was run in two rather than three legs, and since Katie was runner-up in the first and won the second, and Hugo Simon won the first and was runner-up in the second, the two riders finished on equal points and had to jump off for the Cup. Katie won the draw and put Hugo in to jump first. Gladstone sped round clear in a good time, making it imperative for Katie to go both fast and clear. She set off in hot pursuit with the huge bay ex-racehorse, but narrowly failed to beat Hugo's time and took a rail off the second-last fence in the process. It was, however, a tremendous effort for a horse who had shown his outstanding potential very early on by setting a new indoor high-jump record over a 7ft 1in wall at the Washington International Show of 1977 but who had been jumping at top level for less than a year and a half.

Katie with The Jones Boy, whose remarkable recovery from illness astounded the veterinary experts

He and Katie looked set for more international honours, but The Jones Boy was not seen again in Europe and those who had admired him in Gothenburg wondered if it had been simply a flash-in-the-pan performance. The reality was much more tragic. Shortly after returning from Gothenburg, Jonesy fell ill with purpura hemmorhagica, a rare and often fatal allergic condition. Burning with fever and suffering from severely swollen legs and head, Jonesy amazed the vets by surviving at all. But their delight when it became obvious that he was going to pull through quickly turned to dismay. When the swelling subsided the horse's skin began literally to fall away from the worst-affected parts – his hind legs – exposing large areas of raw flesh.

It was only with the help of a human plastic surgeon that skin grafts were laboriously and, against all the odds, successfully applied. A long recuperation period followed, during which it often seemed impossible that the horse would ever sufficiently recover the use of his legs, with their desperately vulnerable covering of new skin, to compete again. That he did is testimony to his own indomitable courage and the skill and dedication of his vets and handlers. It was a triumph for them all when he finally reappeared on the 1982 Florida circuit. In the tough Tampa Grand Prix, he was one of only three horses to get through to the jump-off. To beat the 1981 World Cup winners Michael Matz and Jet Run, he had to go fast and clear. Not since Gothenburg had Katie asked him for such an effort. And to the delight of all his connections, he responded with a clear round that was six-tenths of a second faster than Jet Run's. He was back where he belonged, in the winner's enclosure.

Katie, meanwhile, had also been having a lean time. Jonesy was her only Grand Prix horse at the time and had it not been for George Morris, who stepped in during 1979 and arranged for her to have the ride on Silver Exchange, who belonged to one of his clients, she would have been without an international horse. With Silver Exchange she was selected to ride in the 1980 Rotterdam International Festival ('alternative Olympics'), where the United States team finished fifth. Immediately afterwards, however, the horse was sold by pre-arrangement, and Katie found herself without a top-class ride for the rest of that year and most of the next.

By now she had moved with her family to Virginia and set up her own small establishment, Plain Bay Farm (named after a family joke that every horse she had ever ridden had been a plain bay). It was now possible to have horses at home rather than rely on riding for other stables – but where were these horses to come from? Katie set out with her customary energy to round up a group of buyers and to set off in search of good horses. She found one in Europe: the French-bred stallion Noren, at that time being ridden by Dutchman Johan Heins. Noren had tremendous ability but was known to be a difficult ride, and most people thought that Katie had made a big mistake in buying him. However, she successfully overcame his mouth problems (caused partly by his teeth) and the two became big winners on the Grand Prix circuit. Katie attributes much of her success with Noren to the fact that she did not try to insist that he jump in the flexed, highly collected outline favoured by many European riders. If a horse goes better in a more extended outline, she is happy to accommodate him.

Katie and Make My Day stretch out over the water at Hickstead

California-born Anne Kursinski, double gold medallist in the 1983 Pan American Games, seen here aboard the brilliant Westphalian stallion, Starman

With the advent of Noren, Katie's international career began to take off once again. It reached a high point when she won a World Championship gold medal with Amadia in 1986, the year in which she also won the $250,000 US Cup astride the Hannoverian Special Envoy, became National Champion and got married – to the French rider Henri Prudent (they now have a son). She topped the North American East Coast League of the World Cup in 1982–83 and again in 1987–88 and was runner-up in 1985–86 and 1988–89. With horses such as Jethro, The Governor, Bean Bag, Make My Day and Special Envoy, the eighties brought some spectacular successes for this stylish and dedicated rider.

Career Highlights

1979 World Cup, second place (The Jones Boy)
      World Cup North American League, third place
1983 World Cup North American League, East Coast USA, winner
1986 World Championships, team gold medal (Amadia)
      World Cup North American League, East Coast USA, second place
      National Champion
1988 World Cup North American League, East Coast USA, winner
1989 World Cup North American League, East Coast USA, second place

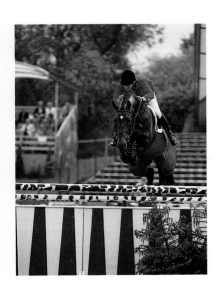

California-born **Anne Kursinski** is one of two American women to have won double gold in the Pan American Games (Mary Chapot [née Mairs] was the first, in 1963). In 1983 in Caracas, riding the Dutch-bred Livius, Anne led the United States team to victory over Canada with a double clear round in the Nations Cup and then defeated the best of the Canadians, Jim Elder, and her team-mate Michael Matz, the defending champion, for the individual gold.

Anne, born on 16 April 1959, started riding lessons at the age of four and a half at the Flintridge Riding Club in Pasadena. Under the expert guidance of Jimmy Williams she became one of the most outstanding riders of hunters and jumpers on the West Coast before moving east in the early eighties. She was reserve rider for the United States at the Los Angeles Olympics, and four years later won a team silver medal in Seoul with the brilliant Westphalian stallion Starman and finished equal fourth indivi-

71

dually together with David Broome and Countryman. She was the only woman rider to complete the individual final. Her Nations Cup successes include two at the end of 1989: Washington, where Starman jumped a double clear, and New York. Based nowadays in New Jersey, Anne is a well-known advocate of protective headgear for riders.

Career Highlights

1982   World Cup North American League, third place
1983   Pan American Games, team and individual gold medals
         (Livius)
1988   Olympic Games, team silver medal (Starman)

Katharine Burdsall's international jumping career took off in a big way in 1986 when she got the ride on the celebrated Hanoverian gelding The Natural, who had changed hands for a record $1 million. This pair were members of the gold medal-winning team at the 1986 World Championships in Aachen. The following year they topped the North American East Coast League of the World Cup and went on to win the final in Paris. Later in that year they won a team silver at the Pan American Games and took the President's Cup at the Washington International Show.

Katharine was born on 17 October 1958 and began riding at the age of six in Connecticut. She trained with George Morris and later with Melanie Smith-Taylor, whose brilliant partnership with the Dutch horse Calypso won her the individual bronze in the 1980 Rotterdam International Festival, the World Cup final in 1982 and a team gold medal at the Los Angeles Olympics. Katharine studied art at the University of Hartford before deciding to concentrate full-time on jumping. Her first top Grand Prix horse was the Dutch-bred Melton Mowbray, and more recently she has been successful with the Holsteiner Toronja.

The million dollar horse The Natural, competing under the pines of Rome with Katharine Burdsall in the saddle

Career Highlights

1986   World Championships, team gold medal (The Natural)
1987   World Cup, winner (The Natural)
         Pan American Games, team silver medal (The Natural)
         World Cup North American League, East Coast USA,
            winner

Leslie Burr-Lenehan, who comes from a theatrical family, chose horses rather than the stage as her career. Here she is riding Normandie at the big Calgary show

Leslie waiting in the wings at West Palm Beach

Leslie Burr-Lenehan is another American woman who routed the Europeans in the World Cup final. Her success came in Gothenburg twelve months before Katharine's Paris victory. Leslie had finished quite a way down the 1985–86 American League and made it to the final only because several of the higher-placed riders dropped out. But the big Oldenburg gelding McLain really rose to the occasion and ran out the winner by the biggest-ever margin, 13 faults ahead of Ian Millar and Big Ben.

Leslie's first top-flight jumper was the ill-fated grey Chase the Clouds (he died of colic in 1982), with whom she enjoyed a lot of success in the late seventies and early eighties. Then came Corsair and Albany, and it was with the latter that she won a team gold medal in the Los Angeles Olympics. (In 1987, when ridden by Deborah Dolan, Albany won, among other things, the Ladies' Championship at Royal Windsor, while on a European tour. Debbie and Albany were the first American pair to win this British Ladies' Championship.) With the thoroughbred Boing, Leslie was in the winning team at the 1983 Pan American Games, and in the late eighties she enjoyed Grand Prix successes with another thoroughbred, Pressurized.

Born on 1 October 1956, Leslie comes from a theatrical family. She is married to fellow rider Brian Lenehan and the couple are based in Connecticut. Like so many of her contemporaries, she owes much of her success to early training with George Morris.

Career Highlights

1980 World Cup North American League, second place
1983 Pan American Games, team gold medal (Boing)
1984 Olympic Games, team gold medal (Albany)
1985 World Cup North American League, East Coast USA,
         third place
         National Champion
1986 World Cup, winner (McLain)

Leslie and the big thoroughbred Pressurized

With so many talented female riders on the circuit, the men certainly do not have it all their own way in the United States. Two who have been at the top longer than most are **Michael Matz** and Joe Fargis. Michael, who was born on 23 January 1951, started riding as a teenager and first competed with the USET in 1973. He was a member of the winning Pan American Games team on three occasions (1975, 1979 and 1983). In 1979 he also took the individual gold with the brilliant Jet Run, the thoroughbred gelding who had also taken the gold in the 1975 Games when ridden by the

74

Michael Matz (left) *and Joe Fargis working in their horses in the Florida sunshine. Both have enjoyed long and successful careers on the international circuit*

Below right: *Michael and Chef at Aachen where they won a team gold medal in the 1986 World Championships*

Below: *Michael Matz and his 1981 World Cup winner Jet Run. Michael is the only rider to have won four gold medals in the Pan American Games*

Mexican Fernando Senderos. Michael is the only rider to have won four gold medals in the Pan American Games.

With Jet Run he represented the USA in the 1978 World Championships, where a double clear in the Nations Cup helped the team win the bronze medal. In the 'change-horse' final, the pair took another bronze. Three years later, in Birmingham, they won the third running of the World Cup final. Other top horses have included Chef and Bon Retour. Michael is married, has two children, and runs a yard in Pennsylvania.

Career Highlights

1975   Pan American Games, team gold and individual bronze medals (Grande)
1978   World Championships, team and individual bronze medals (Jet Run)
1979   Pan American Games, team and individual gold medals (Jet Run)
1981   World Cup, winner (Jet Run)
        World Cup North American League, winner
        National Champion
1983   Pan American Games, team gold and individual bronze medals (Chef)
        National Champion
1984   World Cup North American League, East Coast USA, winner
1986   World Championships, team gold medal (Chef)
1989   National Champion

Joe Fargis, three years Michael's senior, enjoyed a phenomenal run of success in the eighties with two outstanding mares, the thoroughbred Touch of Class, double gold medallist in the Los Angeles Olympics in 1984 and the only horse in Olympic history to jump a double clear round in the Nations Cup, and the Irish-bred Mill Pearl, team silver medallist in Seoul four years later and equal seventh in the individual standings.

Joe was born on 2 April 1948. He has ridden seriously since he was ten years old, when he went to Jane Dillon's Junior Equitation School in Virginia. He trained there until he was in his late teens, becoming an accomplished hunter rider. In 1969 he began studying with the then USET coach Bertalan de Nemethy at the team's training centre in Gladstone, New Jersey. He made his team debut in Europe the following year, helping the United States to win the Nations Cup in Lucerne. Since that time he has been a regular and highly successful member of the American team.

He credits much of his success with jumpers to his early schooling with de Nemethy and to the late Frances N. Rowe, the Virgi-

Joe Fargis and the mare Touch of Class, the first horse to jump two faultless rounds in an Olympic Nations Cup

Four years after Los Angeles, Joe rode another brilliant mare, Mill Pearl, in the Seoul Olympics. They won a team silver medal

nia-based hunter-jumper trainer for whom he rode for many years. Frances Rowe provided the horse Bonte II, for Joe to partner in the 1970 Lucerne Nations Cup; and when Joe went into the army another of her protégés, Conrad Homfeld, took over the ride. It was while they were both working for Frances that Joe and Conrad decided to set up in business together. They have run a training and teaching yard for many years now, first in North Carolina, then in Virginia. In recent times they have operated from Southampton, New York. Joe still competes, while his former team-mate Conrad (whom he defeated for the Los Angeles Olympic gold medal in a jump-off) decided in the late eighties to devote himself to teaching and course building.

In the tough, down-to-earth, professional world of horses, where everything from feeding to riding a line of fences is done with scientific precision, it is reassuring to find, now and again, the odd superstition holding its own with one of the riders. Britain's former National Champion Sue Pountain once attributed her run of success with her popular horse Ned Kelly to her lurid blue nail polish. Conrad Homfeld admitted, after winning his second World Cup in 1985, that he had with him his 'lucky' dollar bill, originally given to him by William Steinkraus to tuck into Abdullah's browband at the Los Angeles Olympics. Steinkraus had had one in his bridle when he had won the individual gold in 1968 and had given one to each of the team members in LA. Conrad says he does not really believe in that sort of thing, but . . . .

Career Highlights

1975   Pan American Games, team gold medal (Caesar)
1984   Olympic Games, team and individual gold medals
        (Touch of Class)
        World Cup North American League, East Coast USA,
          winner
1985   World Cup North American League, East Coast USA,
          winner
1987   World Cup North American League, East Coast USA,
          second place
1988   Olympic Games, team silver medal (Mill Pearl)
        World Cup North American League, East Coast USA,
          third place

*Emma-Jane Mac with her mare,
Oyster, winner of the 1989 Washington
Grand Prix*

Emma-Jane Mac

Y OU MIGHT WELL THINK THAT a horse-mad girl from a wealthy background would have it made in the show-jumping world. Ask dad to buy some tip-top horses, climb aboard and take the sport by storm. Many have tried it. A few have enjoyed some success. Most have found, to their cost, that there is no short cut to the top in the equestrian world, no substitute for miles on the clock, no better way to become a real horseman or horsewoman than learning to ride and school young horses and bring them slowly through the ranks.

Emma-Jane Mac, unlike most of Britain's leading show jumpers, is in the fortunate position of coming from a wealthy family and not needing to go in quest of sponsors to stay in the sport she loves. (Her father, Bill Brown, the chairman of a City insurance brokerage, is reputedly the highest salary earner in the country.) Many girls in her position would have been tempted to ask for the best horses money could buy in the fond belief that they could become stars overnight. But Emma-Jane is much too dedicated a rider to contemplate doing that. She wanted the satisfaction of bringing on novices herself, and set out to learn every aspect of riding and schooling young jumpers. Modest, realistic and professional in her approach, she appreciated from the outset

Above: *Emma-Jane with the hard-pulling Gringo, on whom she won four classes at the 1989 Horse of the Year Show*

that there is no quick way to lasting success in the horse world.

Emma-Jane was born in Essex on 17 March 1964 and, like her older sister Kelly, she was always keen on ponies. After seeing Kelly successfully make the transition to senior competition, Emma-Jane was determined to follow suit. When she left school after taking her O levels she went to work for the late Caroline Bradley, one of the greatest, most respected riders in the world and an acknowledged master of the art of producing young horses. Emma-Jane spent two years with Caroline, learning all she could and doing all the usual stable chores as well as improving her riding. In 1984, the year in which she won the Ladies' National Championship on her sister's ex-ride Guilty, she joined the Everest stable of Liz and Ted Edgar. Since August 1986 she has been based in Hill Wootton, the next village along from the Edgars' Leek Wootton establishment.

When it comes to shopping expeditions for horses, there is no better man to be with than Ted Edgar, and it was while on such a foray to Holland, together with her husband (the 1980 Junior European Champion, Michael Mac), that she found Oyster, now one of her two top rides. That was in March 1987. Six months later Emma-Jane took the six-year-old mare to Wembley, where she won the Foxhunter Championship. Nothing gives a rider, even a top international, more satisfaction than to win this nationwide championship for novice horses, thus proving that all one's hard work and training have been along the right lines.

Oyster was to fulfil her promise in no uncertain terms two seasons later when she won the 1989 Washington Grand Prix with the only double clear round. Emma-Jane's chance to ride with the British team in North America had come about after a brilliantly successful Horse of the Year Show, at which she won four classes on her other top horse Everest Gringo and was consistently in the money on the mare. The Belgian-bred Gringo would not be everybody's idea of the perfect ride for a woman, especially in a cramped indoor arena. He takes a very strong hold, and Emma-Jane admitted after one of those Wembley wins that she was totally out of control going to the last fence. But Gringo's tall, slim rider is happy to settle for this one failing in view of his many good points. 'You can't have everything,' she says realistically, 'and for a big horse – he stands 16.3 hands – he is exceptionally good at turning when jumping against the clock.'

His efforts, and those of his stablemate Oyster, made Emma-Jane the second most successful rider of that 1989 Horse of the Year Show, with £11,764 to her credit. Only John Whitaker did better, mainly because Milton won £27,000 in the International Masters. Emma-Jane's tremendous form deservedly won her a place with the team for Washington, New York and Toronto, and

Gringo tackling one of Hickstead's permanent obstacles

if the Americans and Canadians thought that a British squad without a Whitaker, Skelton, Turi or Broome was very much a second eleven, they were mistaken.

Emma-Jane's victory in the Washington Grand Prix, over a whole host of top United States stars, made her the first British rider ever to win the President of the United States Cup, inaugurated in 1961. It also meant that she had won a World Cup qualifier at her first attempt. Oyster, having been in the Nations Cup team that finished second to the United States at the same show, jumped a brilliant double clear in the New York Nations Cup a week later and the team was unlucky to be beaten, again by the host country, by a mere quarter of a time fault.

In Toronto, however, it was a different story. Emma-Jane (riding Gringo this time), the Smith brothers Robert and Steven, and Peter Charles took the hot favourites, Canada, to a jump-off. Despite the fact that the Canadians were fielding their strongest team, including World Cup winners Ian Millar and Mario Deslauriers, the British quartet sailed to a comfortable victory, and Britain, already assured of the Gucci Trophy for the top team of the year, equalled the record for the highest number (seven) of Nations Cups won by one country in the same season.

Emma-Jane may be able to afford life's luxuries – including an indispensable nanny for her small daughter Jenna – but when it comes to horses she believes in working for her success. Thanks to her sound basic horsemanship and sheer dedication she goes into the nineties as Britain's leading female rider, having overtaken both Liz Edgar and her daughter Marie in the British ranking list. If she fails to maintain that position, it will not be for lack of talent and hard work.

Career Highlights

1984 Ladies' National Champion (Guilty)
1989 Washington Grand Prix (Oyster)
      Toronto Nations Cup, winning team (Gringo)
      Coomes Bookmakers Stakes, International Stakes,
          Wembley Accumulator, Brown Group Speed Horse of
          the Year, Wembley (Gringo)

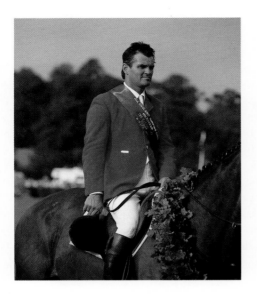

Harvey Smith

'T HERE ISN'T ANOTHER RIDER in the sport who can bring out the best in a horse's performance – and international best at that – in such a short time, even though it may up to then be completely unknown.' Those words, uttered the best part of two decades ago by the now retired five-time Olympic gold medallist Hans Günter Winkler, encapsulated for all time the extraordinary talent which turned builder's son Harvey Smith into one of the most successful riders in show jumping history.

When, during the fifties, he descended from Yorkshire upon the show jumping establishment below – not so much a breath of fresh air, more a whirlwind – it was with a rather plebeian-looking horse called Farmer's Boy who had cost him less than £40 at York Sales. Lack of expensive ponies had not prevented the self-taught lad from Bingley from enjoying a successful junior career and, as a teenager, lack of expensive *horses* was certainly not going to stop him taking on the likes of Steinkraus and the d'Inzeos at the fashionable Royal International.

At the 1958 show, when he was still only nineteen, he won the Young Riders' Championship and (it was this which caused the aficionados' jaws to drop) he was the only British rider to get through to the jump-off for the King George V Gold Cup, in

Above: *Harvey Smith pictured after winning his fourth Hickstead Derby in 1981*

Shining Example, a horse who proved a good servant to Harvey during the eighties

Show jumping is not always a serious business! Harvey takes time off to demonstrate Bal Harbour's latest party trick

which he and Farmer's Boy eventually finished sixth. That performance earned the pair a place in the British team for Dublin, where they duly won the Nations Cup. Harvey's career flourished to such effect that by the end of the eighties he held the record for the British rider with the most Nations Cup wins to his credit: thirty-one (this made him the sixth most successful Cup rider in the history of the sport).

Born on 29 December 1938, Harvey taught himself to ride on his brother's pony. Years later he was to say that he does not care about style: 'I just sit on 'em and pull the strings.' It would not suit everyone, but it certainly worked for Harvey and after he had gained everyone's attention with Farmer's Boy he continued to amaze the world, often with other people's rejects – Warpaint, bought for 200 guineas, being the first of them.

Over the years the list of horses he has ridden reads like a show jumping role of honour: O'Malley, Harvester, Madison Time, Mattie Brown, Summertime, Salvador, Olympic Star, and, during the eighties, a string of horses sponsored by the Japanese company Sanyo who were lumbered rather unfortunately with names such as Sanyo Music Centre and Sanyo Technology which made them, through no fault of their own, rather less memorable to the public. When the Sanyo sponsorship came to an end Harvey, not suprisingly considering the mileage he gives his backers, did not have to wait long for a replacement. Brook Street Bureau, the employment agency, stepped in with a cool half a million to keep the Smith show – Harvey and his two sons Robert and Steven – on the road.

Apart from his outstanding record in Nations Cups, Harvey has in his long career collected a clutch of individual and team medals at European and World Championships, without having actually won a title. He took the individual bronze in the Men's Europeans with O'Malley and Warpaint in 1963 and twice won the individual silver, in 1967 on Harvester and 1971 with Evan Jones and Mattie Brown. He finished third to David Broome in the Men's World Championship in 1970 and won team silvers in the Europeans in both 1977 and 1983, with Olympic Star and Sanyo Olympic Video respectively. He has competed in two Olympic Games, the first in 1968, when he was placed eleventh on Madison Time and the team finished eighth, and the second in 1972, when he rode Summertime in the fourth-placed team but did not start in the individual contest.

Harvey and his younger son Steven out exercising near their Yorkshire home

At home his biggest successes have included four Hickstead Derbies (on Mattie Brown in 1970 and 1971, Salvador in 1974 and Sanyo Video in 1981), seven Grands Prix of Great Britain at the Royal International, the 1970 King George V Gold Cup with Mattie Brown and three National Championships (1960 with Farmer's Boy, 1963 with O'Malley and 1975 with Speakeasy), while his countless overseas triumphs have included the cream of the Grands Prix, such as Rome (O'Malley 1963), New York (O'Malley 1967), Aachen (Graffiti 1977) and Dublin (Mattie Brown 1970, Olympic Star 1976, Sanyo Sanmar 1980, and Sanyo Technology 1983). Equally at home in a speed class, a Derby, a Nations Cup or a Puissance, he has for thirty years been one of the most feared rivals in the jumping arenas of the world.

Look, no horse! Harvey comes back alone after taking a fall at one of the Broome family's Wales and the West shows

Considered by most people the archetypal Yorkshireman – blunt, aggressive, humorous, opiniated, defiant – he has undoubtedly brought show jumping to a far wider audience than it would have attained without his outspoken, often controversial and anti-establishment behaviour. Was any event in the equestrian world more widely reported by the media than his V-sign to Douglas Bunn, Master of Hickstead, in 1971? Has anyone ever been quite so openly and determinedly scornful of the qualifying system for the major British shows? More than thirty years in the sport have done nothing to quieten him when he believes things to be wrong, and he usually manages to have the last laugh.

When he failed to finish high enough up the rider rankings to gain an automatic invitation to Olympia in 1989, he was un-

stinting in his criticism of the system. In the end, as the first rider to have achieved 100 starts in World Cup competitions, he was granted a special 'wild card' invitation by the World Cup director himself, Max Ammann. 'Invitations should go to those capable of winning good classes,' is Harvey's maxim, and having once reached Olympia Harvey lost no time in proving that he *is* still a winner. At the end of that show he retired his winning partner, the gallant old Brook Street Shining Example (affectionately known to everyone as Norman), but waiting in the wings were plenty of good youngsters and the indomitable Harvey had no plans to hang up his boots yet awhile.

Still based in Yorkshire, at a farm at High Eldwick, a stone's throw from Ilkley Moor, where he lives with his second wife Sue (also an accomplished rider), Harvey is as resourceful in middle age as he was in the days of Farmer's Boy. Wrestling and singing, and more recently cabaret, have all come within his compass. He has worked hard to achieve his success and will no doubt go on doing so for years to come. Like him for his honesty, dislike him for his bluntness, it is none the less true that he has helped to give show jumping the sort of popular appeal that all sports need if they are to thrive in this last decade of the twentieth century. Show jumping would have been the poorer without him.

Harvey and Farmer's Boy at the White City in 1958

Career Highlights

1960 National Champion (Farmer's Boy)
1963 Men's European Championship, bronze medal
      (O'Malley/Warpaint)
      National Champion (O'Malley)
1967 Men's European Championship, silver medal
      (Harvester)
1970 Men's World Championship, bronze medal (Mattie Brown)
      King George V Gold Cup (Mattie Brown)
      Hickstead Derby (Mattie Brown)
1971 Men's European Championship, silver medal (Evan Jones/Mattie Brown)
      Hickstead Derby (Mattie Brown)
1974 Hickstead Derby (Salvador)
1975 National Champion (Speakeasy)
1977 European Championships, team silver medal (Olympic Star)
1981 Hickstead Derby (Video)
1983 European Championships, team silver medal (Video)

Robert Smith

Above: *Robert (and friends) at home in Essex. Robert left Yorkshire to set up on his own in 1988*

Robert Smith showing the same determination as his famous father and getting a big jump out of Dictator

A S THE ELDER SON of the redoubtable Harvey Smith, Robert was faced with a daunting task when it came to making a name for himself on the senior circuit. However, at the age of only eighteen he proved that he had no intention of remaining for long in his father's shadow by stealing the King George V Gold Cup at the 1979 Royal International Horse Show from under the very noses of all the leading professionals, including dad, who finished seventh. Robert, who had come of age only the previous month, became the youngest rider ever to win this historic trophy (first contested in 1911). His victory with the brilliant Video resulted in his being selected for the British team to go to Dublin the following month.

That, unfortunately, led to a family row. Harvey, who had been nominated reserve rider for Dublin, declared that if *he* were not given a team place, he would not make his horses available to his son. Robert found himself effectively 'jocked off', as they say in the racing world. Being young, though, he quickly bounced back. He rode Video to win the Grand Prix at the Hickstead Nations Cup meeting, to finish equal second in the Hickstead Derby to the mighty combination of Eddie Macken and Boomerang, and to take the Leading Show Jumper of the Year title at Wembley.

Robert riding Silver Dust at Hickstead

Hardly surprisingly, he soon received a second call to the British team and the autumn saw him embarking, along with father, on the North American 'Fall Circuit' (the international shows at Washington, New York and Toronto). Britain finished fourth, third and equal second respectively in the Nations Cups, Robert having jumped a clear round in each of the first two and a double clear in Toronto. He had, in a few brief months, established himself as one of the most talented of the younger generation of British riders, and events since have done nothing to suggest that his success was a flash in the pan.

Born on 12 June 1961, Robert was, like his younger brother Steven, taught to ride by his father. The boys were put on ponies at an early age, though Harvey has gone on record as saying he was a mite too ambitious on their behalf and could well have put them off riding by expecting too much too soon – other parents beware! On the advice of a friend he substituted a kindly donkey for the ponies, and the ploy worked a treat. The boys soon re-

Riding the ex-David Bowen mount Boysie, Robert won the King George V Gold Cup in 1988 and the valuable Dubai Cup at Hickstead the following year

gained their confidence, later graduated to a Shetland and in due course took to bigger ponies like ducks to water.

Robert's first taste of international success came in the 1977 Junior European Championships in Geneva, when he won a gold medal in the team event and a bronze in the individual (behind France's Eric Navet and Belgium's Véronique Daems-Vastapane, later to become Mrs Michael Whitaker).

As a senior international, many observers feel that Robert has never had quite the horsepower to match his talent, but he has certainly made the best of whatever material has come to hand. In the late eighties he took on David Bowen's former mount Boysie when the horse was well into his teens and had spectacular success with him, scoring a major win in Hannover in late 1987, taking a second King's Cup in 1988 and in 1989 winning the £18,000 Dubai Cup at Hickstead, where he got the better of a thrilling jump-off against the veteran Brazilian star Nelson Pessoa.

Being his father's son, he has on occasion been the subject of controversy. In 1981 he was given a brief suspension by the British Show Jumping Association for misuse of the whip, and in 1987 he was one of the riders (together with Harvey) who, rightly, objected to the poor ground conditions for the National Championship at the Royal Show, refusing to risk his horse unless the fences were re-sited; when the powers that be declined to comply, he helped to move one of the jumps without the consent of the judges. When the competition did finally get under way, Robert won it on Cecil Williams's April Sun. All the riders involved in the fence-moving affair were later fined £300 apiece for conducting themselves 'in a manner which was detrimental to the character and/or prejudicial to the interests of the BSJA'. But the protest had made its point. Not long afterwards the arena was totally re-surfaced.

Although he is Yorkshire born and bred and shares the same sponsors as his father and brother, Robert, with his wife Leanne, has made Saffron Walden, in Essex, his home. Having decided that the time had come to break away from the family set-up, Robert went into partnership with Paul MacAteer in 1988 to open the Quendon Riding Centre, where he is still based.

Career Highlights

1977 Junior European Championships, team gold and
        individual bronze medals (Royal Rufus/Alabama)
1979 King George V Gold Cup (Video)
1987 National Champion (April Sun)
1988 King George V Gold Cup (Boysie)
1989 Dubai Cup (Boysie)

Steven Smith

Above: Steven Smith and Shining Example en route *to winning a team silver medal in the Los Angeles Olympics*

Steven riding the difficult but talented German-bred Picnic at Hickstead in 1989. Later in the year the pair won the Leading Show Jumper title at Wembley

I N 1989 STEVEN SMITH, younger son of Harvey, completed a remarkable and unique family hat-trick at Wembley by winning the Leading Show Jumper of the Year. It was thirty years to the day since the first of his father's three wins in that much-coveted competition, and exactly ten years since that of his older brother Robert. Not surprisingly Harvey, not one given to eulogising over his own riding achievements or those of his sons, was a proud man that day.

Steven's success was the more remarkable in that his partner, Brook Street Picnic, an ex-Paul Shockemöhle horse, is not the easiest of customers to deal with. No one, it seemed, could ride him and he had been rejected as too wayward by, among others, Nick Skelton. In fact it was Nick, who has a much slighter frame than Steven, who had suggested to the more powerfully built Yorkshireman that he should buy him.

Steven took his advice and started riding Picnic at the end of 1988. It was, he admits, certainly *no* picnic. The big German-bred gelding has a propensity for running away – even when he is being led on a headcollar. And if that were not enough, he has a determined and dangerous tendency when being ridden to hang to the left. There were times during the winter when even Steven almost gave up with him. But he found that if he could only cope with the brakes and steering problems, the horse, with his big, careful jump, was a really talented performer. The two were soon going well in good competitions and by the time of his major Wembley success, Picnic had already won back his purchase price. Steven has clearly inherited his father's gift of succeeding with less than ideal equine material.

Born on 22 November 1962, Steven was, like his brother, taught to ride by Harvey when he was very young, but he tended to be less in the limelight than Robert. Until, that is, he was well and truly thrown in the deep end of senior international competition when, at the age of twenty-one, he was selected as a team member for the 1984 Olympic Games in Los Angeles.

Because most of Britain's top riders (including Harvey and Robert) had been obliged to turn professional, the selectors were faced with a difficult task when it came to choosing an Olympic squad. John and Michael Whitaker, who had managed to remain amateurs, were more or less automatic choices, even though Michael had not had nearly as much international experience as John, and Tim Grubb was given the number-three slot. Tim, who had married the American rider Michele McEvoy and settled in the States, had the advantage of being *au fait* with the American jumping scene, and also had a top-class horse in Linky.

Choosing the other two riders to make up the five from whom the Nations Cup team would be chosen was not so easy, since those who were available lacked either international experience or the necessary horsepower. The decision in the end was in favour of David Bowen and Steven. And when Bowen's horses both developed fitness problems, it was Steven who found himself fourth man in the team on the big day at Santa Anita.

Although he had made his senior international debut only the year before, he did have the advantage of the ride on Harvey's good horse Shining Example, not to mention valuable advice from his father, who knew exactly what riding at the Olympics was all about. Harvey, who was doing some commentating for British television, certainly felt the pressure, though. 'It's always worse when it's one of your own,' he says, recalling the nerve-racking battle for the medals in the Nations Cup.

In the first round it was Tim Grubb who pulled out all the stops, providing the British team with their only clear round.

Steven collected 19 faults, three more than John Whitaker and Ryan's Son, and his was the discard score. But things changed dramatically second time round. Linky fell apart, collecting a cricket score of 28.25, and it was Michael Whitaker with Amanda who went clear to keep Britain in the medal hunt. Steven's excellent effort, for just 8 faults, helped significantly in securing the silver, Britain's first Olympic team medal since 1956.

Steven had, as it were, arrived. It was not, however, his first championship medal. He had twice won team gold in the little-publicised Junior European Championships, in Geneva in 1977 and at Stannington the following year, so he was already familiar with the pressures of riding for his country.

When the Smith triumvirate signed their half a million pound sponsorship contract with Brook Street Bureau during the 1987 Horse of the Year Show, it was Steven, in his quiet, unobtrusive way, who took Brook Street's name into the winner's enclosure for the first time by sharing top spot in the Puissance with Vista. Since the Smiths customarily have as many as forty horses at any one time, they can usually find a jumper to suit every class, be it a nippy individual for a scramble against the clock or a 'big wall' specialist.

While Robert has left the Smiths' Yorkshire fold and branched out on his own, Steven is still based with his father at High Eldwick near Bingley, and the two work very much as a team. At least, they do under normal circumstances. Unfortunately, after such a good run of luck in 1989, which culminated in a fine victory with the British team in Toronto, 1990 began very badly for poor Steven. He sustained a seriously broken leg – not, ironically, in a fall from a horse but in a motorbike accident – and was unable to ride for many months while he underwent bone-graft operations.

Career Highlights

1977   Junior European Championships, team gold medal
       (Alabama)
1978   Junior European Championships, team gold medal
       (Sunningdale)
1984   Olympic Games, team silver medal (Shining Example)
1989   Leading Show Jumper of the Year (Picnic)

Nelson Pessoa

WATCHING NELSON PESSOA ATTACK a jump-off course against the clock with all the verve, nerve and flair of a twenty-year-old, it is difficult to believe that he is now in his mid fifties. The oldest rider regularly competing at top international level, he has plotted a lone course round the world's jumping arenas for thirty-five years – lone, because he is the only Brazilian to have uprooted himself from South America and based himself in Europe long term.

Born in Rio de Janeiro on 16 December 1935, Nelson showed such exceptional talent at home that he was selected to ride for his country in the 1956 Stockholm Olympics when he was only twenty. His mount was an unprepossessing little grey horse called Relincho. With double-figure scores in both rounds, he finished in thirty-third place out of the sixty-six starters (better, nevertheless, than either of his older team-mates) and Brazil was placed tenth of the twenty teams.

However, a few weeks later Europe was to see a hint of the burgeoning Pessoa talent when, continuing their European tour, the South Americans sprang a big surprise in Aachen, beating the crack German team – which included two members of the Olympic gold medal-winning trio – in the Nations Cup. It was Nelson

Above: Nelson and his Derby specialist Gran Geste, three times winner at Hamburg and twice at Hickstead

The evergreen Brazilian ace Nelson Pessoa riding Special Envoy at Aachen

95

and Relincho who recorded the best score, and they went well again at London's White City a couple of weeks later where the team finished runners-up to Britain.

Encouraged by these successes, the Brazilians returned to Europe the following year. Their placings included a second behind the Germans in Aachen and a third in Paris, and always it was Nelson who put up the most outstanding performances (including a double clear in Lisbon). For the next three years he continued to campaign from his home country, but he already knew that if he was to achieve his ambition of making a career out of show jumping he would have to live nearer to the centre of the action.

Accordingly, from 1961 he began spending his summers in Switzerland, at Vandoeuvres, so that he could compete in earnest throughout Europe. Riding his own horses and those of fellow Brazilian Arline Givaudan, whose yard became one of the most formidable on the Continent, he quickly established himself as one of the world's most successful show jumpers.

Thanks to his unique talent for spotting good young horses and his unsurpassed gifts as a trainer and rider, he has remained at the top year in year out and is always a dangerous adversary, whether he is tackling a Puissance, a Derby or a Grand Prix. With Madame Givaudan's Huipil – the horse on which she had finished runner-up in the 1963 Ladies' European Championships at Hickstead – he was placed equal fifth in the 1964 Olympics. Teaming up Huipil with his own athletic little grey Brazilian-bred gelding Gran Geste, who still holds the record for the most wins in the tough Hamburg Derby (three), he was runner-up the following year in the Men's European Championship and in 1966 won the title.

It was to be his last tilt at the European Championship, which that year had seen all three medals go to non-European riders: the silver had been won by Frank Chapot of the USA and the bronze by Argentina's Hugo Arrambide. Realising the ridiculousness of this situation, the FEI decided that it would not, in future, permit non-Europeans to compete simply because they were based in Europe at the time.

In the Men's World Championship, staged that same year in Buenos Aires, Nelson upheld the honour of South America by qualifying for the change-horse final with Huipil, but sadly finished out of the medals. However, there was swift recompense for the Brazilian star in the Americas' own continental championship, the Pan American Games, in 1967. Riding Gran Geste, Nelson jumped a double clear round to lead Brazil to victory in the team event and went on to win the individual silver.

In 1974 he decided to turn professional, and since then he has ridden a succession of good horses for his sponsors, Moët et Chandon, among them the brilliant Puissance mare Miss Moët, who at the 1983 Paris CSIO cleared the wall at 7ft 7¾in (2.33 metres), an unofficial record which was to stand for several years. Always a force to be reckoned with on the indoor World Cup circuit, too, 'Neco', as he is known, has enjoyed much success with Fil d'Argent, Sans Pardon, Larramy and, most recently, the Irish-bred Special Envoy (not to be confused with Katie Monahan-Prudent's ride of the same name), all with the Moët et Chandon prefix.

After having moved to France in the late sixties, he changed country yet again in the eighties and is now based permanently in Belgium. He is married with a teenage son, Rodrigo, who has clearly inherited his father's remarkable equestrian talent. With good horses to ride and the invaluable guidance of his father, Rodrigo looks certain to keep the Pessoa name at the forefront of show jumping long after Nelson has retired from the fray.

Career Highlights

1956 National Champion
1958 National Champion
1959 Pan American Games, team silver medal (Copacabana)
1960 National Champion
1962 Hamburg Derby (Espartaco)
1963 Hamburg Derby (Gran Geste)
      Hickstead Derby (Gran Geste)
1964 Aachen Grand Prix (Gran Geste)
1965 Men's European Championship, silver medal (Huipil/ Gran Geste)
      Hamburg Derby (Gran Geste)
      Hickstead Derby (Gran Geste)
1966 Men's European Championship, gold medal (Huipil/ Gran Geste)
1967 Pan American Games, team gold and individual silver medals (Gran Geste)
1968 Hamburg Derby (Gran Geste)
1984 World Cup, equal second place (Larramy)

Eddie Macken

EDDIE MACKEN, THE SUPREME STYLIST, will go down in sporting history not just as one of the greatest riders to come out of Ireland but as one of the greatest riders of all time in the world. There is in his riding that harmonious blend of strength, delicacy, elegance and dash which singles out the truly great horseman.

Eddie's remarkable talents first became evident to a wide audience in the early seventies when he started competing at championship level on horses owned by the renowned former international rider turned teacher, Iris Kellett. They came to full fruition when he teamed up with one of the greatest horses who ever looked through a bridle: Boomerang.

Eddie was born in Granard, County Longford, on 20 October 1949. The youngest of five children, he was encouraged to ride by his father, Jimmy, an enthusiastic hunting man who also did some point-to-pointing. There was never a time when ponies and horses were not a part of young Eddie's life. He competed with great success as a junior jumper and then, at the age of eighteen, moved up into the big league, to the Dublin yard of Iris Kellett.

By the time he was ready to compete in his first championship, the 1973 Europeans at Hickstead, word had begun to spread that the young Irishman had an exceptional talent. Neither of the

horses he was riding at that time, Oatfield Hills and Easter Parade, was of true championship class, and Eddie could finish only ninth behind Paddy McMahon and Pennwood Forge Mill. But it was valuable match experience and at the following year's Men's World Championship, also at Hickstead, Eddie came close to taking the title from under the noses of some of the most experienced riders of the day.

Riding Iris Kellett's former show hunter Pele, whose sheer brilliance outweighed his inexperience (he was only a seven-year-old), Eddie won the first leg of the championship, was equal first in the second and equal second in the third. He went into the change-horse final together with Hartwig Steenken on the wonder mare Simona, Hugo Simon on Lavendel and Frank Chapot, veteran of the United States team, on Main Spring. Eddie and Hartwig collected only 4 faults apiece (both, oddly enough, with Main Spring) and so had to jump off for the title. Drawn first, the young Irishman, knowing the prowess of the mare, was forced to hurry in an effort to set an unbeatable time. Pele collected 8 faults. Hartwig, gambling on a slow clear, collected 4 faults at the water and was twenty seconds slower, but victory was his.

But even though he missed the title, that championship set the seal on Eddie's career. He had caught the eye of, among others, the German owner Dr Schnapka (Simona was just one of his many top-class horses). Eddie, realising the advantages to be gained by being based in mainland Europe rather than in his native country, accepted the chance to go to live in Mühlen, base of the Schockemöhle brothers. He turned professional and proceeded to gain valuable experience campaigning on the tough European circuit.

Boomerang's reappearance in his life was to make him one of the most successful riders of all time. By the thoroughbred stallion Battleburn, out of a hunter mare, Boomerang had, ironically, been in Iris Kellett's yard when Eddie was there. Ted Edgar bought him for Liz to ride as a five-year-old in 1972, and although he did not have the best mouth in the world he was clearly a horse with great potential. It was only because he began to have trouble with his feet (he was subsequently denerved) that the Edgars decided in 1973 to accept one of the many offers they received for him. He was sold to Dutchman Leon Melchior and later to Paul Schockemöhle, who wanted him as a speed horse for himself. Ultimately Dr Schnapka acquired him, and as soon as Eddie started riding him it became obvious that he was going to be more than just a speed horse.

When Eddie later returned to live in Ireland – he, his wife Suzanne and their two children are based nowadays at Kells in County Meath – Boomerang went with him; and since Eddie was

Previous page: *Genius at work: Eddie Macken and his horse of a lifetime, Boomerang, jumping at Dublin*

The irreplaceable Boomerang, one of the greatest Grand Prix and Derby horses of all time

also reunited with Pele, now renamed Kerrygold, who had been ridden in his absence by Paul Darragh, he had a formidable duo with which to contest the big international events. In the 1977 European Championships he opted to ride the rather more experienced Kerrygold and although he got off to a bad start in the first competition, he caught up in the second and took Dutchman Johan Heins with the Welsh-bred Seven Valleys to a jump-off. Both riders collected 4 faults and Eddie lost the title by a tenth of a second.

Twelve months later in Aachen he had a second crack at the world title, this time on Boomerang. But the fates were determined, once again, to deprive him of a title by the narrowest of margins. In the change-horse final, the German rider Gerd Wiltfang rode four clear rounds. So, too, did Eddie – except for a quarter of a time fault on Johan Heins's horse Pandur Z. To lose two championships in jump-offs and a third by a time fault would be enough to depress even the most resilient of spirits; but with Boomerang to ride, no one could be downhearted for long. Four consecutive Hickstead Derbies is a record which looks likely to remain unbeaten for a very long time indeed, and he was one of the most prolific Grand Prix winners of all time.

A horse of the calibre of Boomerang usually comes only once in a lifetime, and since his retirement in 1980 Eddie has had his share of those lean patches which many riders experience as they seek to replace a brilliant partner with new young ones. Throughout the eighties the horses he rode for his long-time sponsors, Carrolls, were useful rather than brilliant. They included Royal Lion, Onward Bound and Wendy.

Then in 1987 he teamed up with the Westphalian mare Welfenkrone, whose German owner was based at a stud in Ireland. Welfenkrone won the Olympia Grand Prix that year in fine style and Eddie had high hopes of her as an Olympic horse. Having turned professional so early in his career he had never had the opportunity to ride in the Games, but under the new rules he regained 'competitor' status and could have gone to Seoul. But Eddie's championship bad luck dogged him once again. The mare injured herself during the summer while being loaded up after a show. Since his stallion, Flight, was also sidelined through injury not long afterwards, Eddie had to miss the Games.

The eighties ended on a sober note for Ireland's most famous rider when Carrolls, staunch supporters of Irish show jumping for some twelve years, decided to pull out of sports sponsorship with the exception of golf. But with a horse as talented as Welfenkrone in his yard, it is unlikely that we have seen the last of the riding genius of Eddie Macken.

Eddie brings Kerrygold down the Hickstead Derby bank in perfect style

Eddie riding Royal Lion

Career Highlights

1974   Men's World Championship, silver medal (Pele)
1976   Hamburg Derby (Boomerang)
       Hickstead Derby (Boomerang)
       New York Grand Prix (Boomerang)
1977   European Championships, individual silver medal
         (Kerrygold, formerly Pele)
       Hickstead Derby (Boomerang)
       Brussels Grand Prix (Boomerang)
1978   World Championships, individual silver medal
         (Boomerang)
       Hickstead Derby (Boomerang)
       Gothenburg Grand Prix (Boomerang)
       Rome Grand Prix (Boomerang)
       Aachen Grand Prix (Boomerang)
       Aachen Championship (Boomerang)
       Hamburg Derby (Boy)
1979   European Championships, team bronze medal
         (Boomerang)
       World Cup, equal third place (Carrolls of Dundalk)
       Hickstead Derby (Boomerang)
       Royal International Horse Show, John Player Trophy
         (Boomerang)
       Calgary Grand Prix (Boomerang)
1980   Millstreet Derby (Onward Bound)
1981   Hamburg Derby (Spotlight)
1984   Gothenburg Grand Prix (El Paso)

Annette Miller

Vivacious, articulate and bubbling with enthusiasm, Annette Miller would, one feels, be a success at whatever she turned her hand to. With an aerobatic style all of her own and an equine partner, Tutein, to match her effervescent personality, she brought a welcome breath of fresh air to the world of British show jumping during the eighties. Win or lose, the public loves her for her entertainment value. But she is much more than just a likeable personality. Her flamboyant style may be amusing to watch, but beneath it there is that same determined will to win that inspires all those of her rivals who cut less of a dash in the ring.

It was at Hickstead in 1984 that Annette (unintentionally) first caught the public's attention in a big way. A huge live crowd and millions of TV viewers watched in horror as she rode her flying grey Tutein, never one to lack forward impulsion, a trifle too energetically on to the formidable Derby Bank. The big-hearted gelding, quite misunderstanding what was wanted, came to the steep descent and simply launched himself straight off the top instead of sliding down. Hardly surprisingly he crumpled in a heap on landing, dropping his young rider on the hallowed Hickstead turf before galloping off towards the exit. The pair, left on opposite sides of the arena, were eliminated for not continuing the course within the statutory time allowance.

Annette admits that on her next visit to the Derby meeting she was not enthusiastic about taking part. However, she and Tutein won the Derby trial, which automatically qualified her for the big event, and with so much pressure on her to take part, she gave way. This time Tutein made his descent in a more traditional manner.

Two years after that, however, the pair again provided the

drama in the Derby when, approaching the last fence in 1988, Annette's reins broke and Tutein galloped clean past the jump out of control. To lose brakes and steering is a rider's nightmare in any event, but particularly so on a forward going horse in the vast open spaces of Hickstead's international arena. Nothing daunted, quick-thinking Annette leaned forward to grab hold of the cheek-piece of the bridle, pulled him round in a circle and, showing incredible coolness, tackled the oxer again to complete the course. Stopping was not so easy, but her team of helpers was quickly at hand to apprehend the runaway grey, and fortunately everyone escaped unscathed.

'Team' is a word which always comes to mind when one thinks of Annette, for her success has been and still is very much a family affair. Her parents, Shirley and Alan Lewis, sold their bakery business in London's East End to enable their children to have first ponies, then horses on which to compete. The Lewises are first-generation horse owners, Alan having been initiated into things equestrian when he was evacuated from London to a farm in 1939. Years later he paid a café-owner client £50 for the family's first pony, setting the name Lewis on the path to show jumping glory. Although Shirley has never ridden, Alan used to go hunting and can still occasionally be persuaded to climb into the saddle.

Annette, born on 7 October 1964, is the youngest of four children, all of whom were keen pony riders. Jacqueline, now married with two children, no longer competes, and although he occasionally comes out of retirement, brother Anthony is virtually fully employed as the 'man on the ground' for his two younger sisters Annette and Michelle (the latter being two years the senior), both of whom have become internationals. It was Michelle who did much of the early work with the star of the Lewis/Miller string, Tutein, a Dutch-bred horse who probably gets his speed from his grandsire, the well-known flat racehorse Abernant. Michelle and Tutein won a team gold medal in the 1981 Junior European Championships. Three years later Tutein carried Annette to a team silver in the Young Riders Europeans.

With the family favourite Tutein now well into his teens, Annette will be concentrating more and more on her rising young star Zephyrus. Although both horses are greys, there the similarity ends. Tutein, who actually stands 16.1 hands, looks smaller, probably because of his thoroughbred ancestry and bouncy style of jumping. Zephyrus, also Dutch-bred, is well over 17 hands and an altogether more substantial type. Whereas Tutein could win the Speed Horse of the Year title one minute and jump a Grand Prix course the next, Zephyrus will be at his best, Annette feels, in Nations Cups. As back-ups to the two greys the Lewises have Teadies and Supergrass, and are always looking for more talented

Previous page: The distinctive style of Annette Miller, seen here riding Tutein

youngsters.

A proud moment for Annette after receiving a prize in Stockholm from the King of Sweden

Married since August 1989 to sports osteopath James Miller (whom she met, appropriately, at Hickstead), Annette lives at Bishop's Stortford, where James has one of his two practices, and she commutes daily to the family home at Chigwell Row in Essex, still the base for the horses. She clearly enjoys being a housewife and loves cooking, though she says she is getting a bit long in the tooth for her erstwhile favourite pastime, dancing!

When she has time Annette likes to do a bit of training, and she is particularly good with ponies and their riders. She does not, she hastens to add, teach them to ride in her own distinctive style. Her habit of kicking her legs up in the air over a fence originated, she believes, when she was very young. She was so tall for her age – 5ft 4in at ten – that her father always had to take her birth certificate to shows to prove she was still young enough to compete with small ponies. She recalls that on 12.2s her feet virtually met under the girth and she acquired the habit of kicking her legs back to avoid hitting fences. Since then she has tried to cure the habit by tying her stirrups to the girth, but that practice had to be abandoned because of an FEI rule forbidding it.

Nowadays she has stopped trying to ride in any other way, though she feels that she does sit rather differently on the big Zephyrus, simply because he has a different approach to jumping from Tutein. People still criticise, sometimes saying that she looks ridiculous when she is jumping. And that, she admits, hurts. (Her critics have perhaps forgotten, or are too young to remember, the not dissimilar styles of riders such as Alan Oliver and Ted Edgar – who were not exactly unsuccessful). The most important thing is that Annette's style works for her and has made her popular with audiences both at home and abroad. And that can only be good for the sport.

Career Highlights

1984   Young Riders European Championships, team silver medal (Tutein)

1985   Lisbon Nations Cup, winning team (Tutein)
Young Show Jumper of the Future Award (Falcon H)

1986   Hickstead Derby Trial (Tutein)

1987   Brown Group Speed Horse of the Year, Wembley (Tutein)
Modern Alarms Snowman Stakes, Olympia (Tutein)

1988   Ladies' National Champion (Tutein)
Modern Alarms Snowman Stakes, Olympia (Tutein)

Philip Heffer

PHILIP HEFFER WAS SIX WHEN his father decided, as a joke, to book some riding lessons for himself and a customer from his business in the wholesale meat trade. The experiment was not a success and after the two men had fallen off a couple of times they decided that equestrian sport was not for them. But it seemed a pity to waste the pre-arranged lessons, so Philip and his older brother Mark started riding in their place. And that is how, purely by accident, the Heffer family took its first faltering steps towards equestrian fame.

Philip, born in Essex on 18 January 1966, is the second of the Heffers' five children (he has two younger brothers and a sister), all of whom climbed on to ponies in due course. Mark, two years Philip's senior, achieved international success as a pony rider when, partnering Frère Jacques, he helped Britain take the team silver medal in the Pony European Championships of 1979. In the following two years Philip rode this brilliant pony with the team, collecting gold each time, on the second occasion with a double clear round.

In 1983 Philip was in the team which finished just out of the medals in the next step up the ladder, the Junior European Championships. His mount was Valley View, the horse on whom Mark

Philip Heffer and Viewpoint at Hickstead. Philip's greatest ambition is to win the Derby there

had won a team gold in 1981. Although he failed to bring home a medal on that occasion, 1983 was nevertheless a most significant year in Philip's career, for it was that season that he acquired from Andy Austin the horse with whom he was to shoot to fame in senior international competition: Viewpoint, at that stage a six-year-old and only £1.00 into Grade A.

Philip rode him in the Junior Europeans in 1984, when once again the British team finished fourth, this time after a jump-off with France. The pair finished the season by taking the Young Riders Championship at Wembley. The following year they made their senior Nations Cup debut and Philip proved that he was more than ready to take on the top stars by winning the prestigious Rotterdam Grand Prix. A few weeks later he and Viewpoint jumped a brilliant double clear in the Young Riders European Championships, clinching Britain's second team gold in that event, before rounding off the season in tremendous style by finishing third in the World Cup Qualifier at Olympia.

Philip rides with great élan and is never seen to better effect than when contesting a jump-off against the clock, when he makes full use of Viewpoint's ground devouring stride without losing control of his hard-pulling partner. Over the years he has had the benefit of coaching from Geoff Glazzard, and more recently, David Broome's sister Mary has helped iron out Viewpoint's problems.

Despite his terrific jumping ability, the bay gelding's progress to the top has not been without its difficulties. A few seasons ago he started to refuse when a spell of back trouble undermined his confidence. Even after his back was put right, memories of that bad time led him to go on refusing for fear of incurring more pain. Patient schooling from Mary helped convince him that all was well and during 1988 he showed clear signs that he was starting to come right again. By 1989 he was back at the top, winning the Grand Prix at Eindhoven, the Swedish Jumping Derby in Falsterbo, and finishing runner-up in the Olympia World Cup Qualifier, in which he had the satisfaction of beating the time set by John Whitaker and Milton.

However, Philip's most satisfying achievement of the eighties was without doubt jumping a clear round in the 1989 Hickstead Derby. Ever since he was a boy, he has dreamed of winning that marathon event, and he admits that it was very disappointing to jump one of the very rare clear rounds, only to find himself finishing third in a jump-off with two others who did the same.

Based now at Sacombe Green, in Hertfordshire, Philip has been married to fellow show jumper Jane Richards since early 1990, and it is his wife who manages the running of the yard while Philip continues to earn his living in the family meat business.

Viewpoint jumping with all his usual zest at Stockholm in 1989. By that time he had overcome the back problems which had beset him a couple of seasons previously

Philip pictured after winning the Swedish Jumping Derby on Viewpoint

The pattern for him is to work all day in Romford and to ride when he gets home in the afternoon. During the winter he does more work and less riding; during the summer it is the other way around. He says he is lucky that there are four members of the family involved in the firm, which makes it possible for him to take time off during the rest of the year to continue competing. His brother Mark, incidentally, who chose catering as his profession, has given up competitive riding.

Viewpoint continues to head Philip's string of half a dozen horses, and he has high hopes of an Oldenburg mare called Vanessa whom he acquired in Germany at the end of 1989. One of them, he hopes, will help him fulfil his long cherished ambition of winning that coveted Hickstead Derby. If there were time to spare after work and riding, Philip would like to be involved in other sports – he particularly enjoys football, golf and squash – but for the foreseeable future horses look likely to dominate his life.

Career Highlights

1980   Pony European Championships, team gold medal (Frère Jacques)
1981   Pony European Championships, team gold medal (Frère Jacques)
1984   Whitbread Young Riders Championship (Viewpoint)
1985   Rotterdam Grand Prix (Viewpoint)
        Young Riders European Championships, team gold medal (Viewpoint)
1986   Young Riders European Championships, team silver medal (Viewpoint)
1989   Eindhoven Grand Prix (Viewpoint)
        Hickstead Derby, third place (Viewpoint)
        Falsterbo Derby (Viewpoint)

Hugo Simon

THE DIMINUTIVE FIGURE OF HUGO SIMON aboard powerfully built German-bred horses such as Fair Lady, Landgräfin and, above all, Gladstone became one of the most popular attractions to show jumping audiences during the seventies and eighties – nowhere more so than in Sweden, where he commanded the sort of adulation usually accorded only to pop stars. However, beneath the outwardly flamboyant style of riding that has made him such a favourite with the public lies a wealth of training in the correct principles of dressage, and it is a tribute to his horsemanship that the always highly strung Gladstone would stand rock still in the entrance tunnel to the *Scandinavium* stadium in Gothenburg facing a deafening barrage of cheering and stamping from a 12,000-strong crowd and then go in and jump a clear round.

Hugo, who was born in and competes for Austria, acquired his riding skills in Germany. Born on 3 August 1942, he moved to Germany with his parents when he was three. His father was a dealer and breeder and Hugo began riding, on a small Arab horse, when he was eight. Within a year he was champion of the district where he lived, a position he retained for six years. He made his international debut when he was fifteen and for several years took

Above: *Hugo Simon*

Hugo Simon and Gladstone, individual gold medallists at the 1980 Rotterdam International Festival

113

winter courses at the renowned German training centre Warendorf, where he rode dressage under the tutelage of Olympic rider Harry Boldt's father. During this time he competed in international dressage events before returning to show jumping.

Partnering the brilliant Hanoverian mare Fair Lady, Hugo was by 1971 one of the most successful riders in Germany, and quite reasonably hoped for selection to the 1972 Olympic team. He was, however, overlooked. Deeply disappointed, but not one to give up without a fight, and secure in the knowledge that he had a horse of Olympic calibre, he applied for permission to ride for Austria (claiming dual nationality through his Austrian grandmother), turning down in the meantime a request to lend Fair Lady to the German team. His plans seemed to be progressing well until a month before the Munich Games, when Fair Lady broke down.

Since his other top horse, the grey Lavendel, was only a youngster, the Austrian Federation said they wished to see him finish in the first three in the Grands Prix at La Baule and Dinard before agreeing to send him to Munich. Lavendel obliged, taking third place in both competitions, and the pair duly lined up for the Olympic individual contest. Hugo's performance speaks for itself. Along with German team gold medallist Hartwig Steenken on Simona and Canada's Jim Day on Steelmaster, he missed the jump-off for the medals by a mere three-quarters of a time fault and was placed equal fourth. Not unnaturally it gave him great satisfaction that no German rider finished higher than he did.

Lavendel proved a good servant to Hugo, finishing fifth in the 1973 European Championships, equal third in the 1974 World championships, fourth in the 1975 Europeans and equal fifth in the 1976 Olympics. Later he proved a valuable schoolmaster for Hugo's daughter Cornelia who, together with her younger brother Karl Phillip, began riding at an early age and was accompanied on the junior show circuit by Hugo's then wife, Gabi.

It was in 1978 that Hugo took over the ride on the difficult but hugely talented Gladstone. This big Hanoverian gelding was only five and a half when he won his first Grand Prix with Hartwig Steenken, at Paris in 1975, and it was a partnership which looked to have a great future. But in July 1977 tragedy struck. The German star sustained injuries in a car crash from which he never recovered. He died the following January, aged thirty-six, without having regained consciousness.

Gladstone, who more than fulfilled his early promise, was to prove Hugo's most successful horse, taking him to gold medals in the first World Cup Final in 1979 (the only European winner in the first eleven runnings of that championship) and in the 1980 Rotterdam International Festival, staged for those countries

Gladstone, ridden by Hartwig Steenken until his untimely death in 1978, made Hugo Simon one of the most successful riders in the world

Winzer, a Hanoverian gelding acquired by Hugo after he lost the ride on The Freak and other horses owned by Dr Batliner

114

Hugo riding The Freak. The horse was later sold to the German rider Dirk Hafemeister and won a team gold medal at the Seoul Olympics

which boycotted the Moscow Olympics. Two days after seeing a possible team gold dwindle to a bronze when Gladstone hit two fences in the second round of the Nations Cup, Hugo had the horse back at his unsurpassable best for the individual title. Drawn last of the three in the jump-off for the medals, and knowing that both Melanie Smith with Calypso and John Whitaker with Ryan's Son had each collected 4 faults, Hugo, not one to crack under pressure, opted to go for a safe, slow clear round. His brave gamble paid off. This time he was glad to have earned three-quarters of a time fault, for Gladstone cleared the massive fences faultlessly. But for the intervention of politics, Hugo would surely have gone down in the record books as an Olympic champion.

Although Gladstone went on jumping with great success until 1986 – particularly in World Cup finals, a competition of which Hugo is very much in favour – by the time of the Los Angeles Olympics in 1984 his rider already had a new rising star in his string, The Freak. Bred in Holland by the same stallion as Calypso (Lucky Boy), The Freak finished in equal twenty-second place in Los Angeles at the age of only eight, made rapid progress thereafter and at the 1986 World Cup final, the show at which Gladstone was officially retired, took a creditable sixth place.

Then came the second big drama of Hugo's career. Towards the end of that year the European circuit was buzzing with the news that Hugo and his long-time owner, the Liechtensteiner Doctor Batliner, had had a disagreement and were parting company. The dispersal of horses was swift. Of the best, the mare Landgräfin, rated at one time by Hugo as superior to Gladstone, was retired to stud, Gräfin was retained for Dr Batliner's son to ride, and Dirk Hafemeister acquired The Freak, who was to prove his worth by winning a team gold medal at the Seoul Olympics in 1988 when ridden, as a last minute substitute for a lame horse, by Ludger Beerbaum.

The situation called for all Hugo's fighting qualities if he was to retain his position on the international circuit. With his customary energy he wasted no time in securing the ride on some new horses, and if they were not of quite the quality of The Freak, they kept him in circulation throughout the latter part of the eighties. He rode the grey Hanoverian Winzer into ninth place in the 1987 World Cup final and took Gypsy Lady, another grey Hannoverian, to the Seoul Olympics. Showing his usual determination, he qualified this relatively inexperienced eight-year-old for the individual final, but on the big day she took exception to the double of water ditches, depositing Hugo unceremoniously into the first one. Bedraggled but typically still smiling, Hugo eventually decided to call it a day.

It is not, however, in Hugo's nature to call it a day for long, and

Hugo in his Superman costume – his fans in Gothenburg went wild when he wore it in the fancy dress competition

the search goes on for the sort of horses he likes best – those with the same fighting spirit as his own. Keen on sports as diverse as skiing and tennis, he has kept himself fit despite the passing of the years (on one memorable occasion not so long ago he accepted the challenge of jumping a Puissance wall without a horse, and won the large quantity of wine on offer by pole vaulting over!). If his Swedish fans have any say in the matter, it will be many years before they are forced to put away their banners declaring their undying devotion to one of the sport's greatest showmen.

Career Highlights

1974   Men's World Championship, bronze medal (Lavendel)
1979   World Cup, winner (Gladstone)
         World Cup European League, second place
1979   European Championships, individual bronze medal
         (Gladstone)
1980   International Show Jumping Festival, Rotterdam,
         individual gold and team bronze medals (Gladstone)
         World Cup European League, second place
1981   World Cup, third place (Gladstone)
1982   World Cup, equal third place (Gladstone)
1983   World Cup, second place (Gladstone)
1985   National Champion
1988   National Champion

Hugo besieged by enthusiastic young Swedish fans at Gothenburg, where he enjoys tremendous popularity

Peter Murphy

THE FLAIR WITH WHICH PETER MURPHY rode his way to two European championship titles while still in his teens marked him out very early on as an outstanding young rider. Today, just turned twenty-one, he is regarded as one of the most exciting prospects to emerge on the British show jumping scene for many years.

Peter was born in Lancashire on 18 June 1969. His father died when he was only four but his mother, Diana, remarried – her husband, Bob Astill is in the saddlery retail business – and there was always plenty of family encouragement for Peter and his three sisters when it came to ponies. A born rider, he never had any formal tuition at a riding school but learned the basics of good horsemanship from his parents. His mother attributes his marvellous sense of balance to the fact that at one time, when he was very small, he insisted on riding bareback. His parents would put a saddle on his pony, only for him to take it off again immediately and go careering round the field over a series of little jumps!

It was not long, however, before the aspiring young show jumper was content to ride in the conventional manner. He began competing at Pony Club level when he was seven, and a year later graduated to affiliated jumping. He showed such tremendous competitive prowess that he was selected to jump in Dublin at the age of nine and won the 12.2-hands championship there.

Owners of top-class ponies were soon offering him rides, which was how he came to team up with such brilliant performers as Foxlynch Little John and The Welshman. In 1983, not long after his fourteenth birthday, he won his first championship medal, a team gold in the Pony Europeans, riding his own pony Mr Punch. The following year he took the individual title and a team silver with Foxlynch Little John, and twelve months later the pair won another team gold and took the individual silver. Remarkably, in all three championships Peter scored a double clear round in the Nations Cup. He rounded off 1985 by finishing first and second in the Leading Junior Show Jumper of the Year at Wembley and winning the National Grade C Championship, demonstrating that the switch from ponies to horses was going to cause him no problems whatsoever.

Like Nick Skelton before him, Peter had at one time entertained the thought of going into racing, and just before he left school he spent a month in stables. His mother admits that she was frankly alarmed at the prospect of her son becoming a National Hunt jockey – he was already too heavy to ride on the flat. But although he enjoyed those weeks spent with racehorses, she need not have worried. His heart was clearly in show jumping and it was to his first love that he soon returned.

After leaving school in 1985 he set about establishing himself on the senior circuit, riding his own mare Leamlara and several horses for other owners, notably Stanley Whittaker's Jay's Way. It was with this grey gelding that he was selected to ride in the 1987 Junior European Championships, which are open to riders up to eighteen years of age. The atrocious weather conditions in Belgium caused Britain to withdraw from the team contest, but Jay's Way battled valiantly through the mud to give Peter his second individual title in four years and the greatest international success of his teenage career. Later in the year he won the Young Rider of the Year at Wembley with PPD.

Despite the lack of any substantial financial backing, Peter has, through his own dedication and determination, supported by the enthusiastic help of his family, worked his way steadily up the riders' ranking list (based on points according to the amount of prize money a rider has won). During 1989 alone he pulled up ten places, from twenty-sixth to sixteenth.

Qualifying for the limited places available at Britain's three big indoor shows – the Royal International, Wembley and Olympia – is not easy, and the different systems employed have inevitably come in for their fair share of criticism. But Peter, by the age of twenty, had proved that young riders *can* get their foot

Peter's remarkable record in under-21 championships led to his being taken on as stable jockey by senior team manager Ronnie Massarella

in the door if they have sufficient talent and are prepared to work hard.

Wembley, where the criterion is prize money won during the year, opened its doors to him as a senior rider in 1988. Olympia, based partly on the riders' standings in the FEI computer list and partly on appearances with the British team abroad, he cracked the following year. The Royal International, for which entry is based partly on the British riders' ranking list, with other places going to those with sufficient points earned in Area International

121

Trials, he considers the least satisfactory system, though one which is acceptable until someone comes up with a better idea. If you are not in the top ten on the list, then you simply have to do well in AITs. With a little way to go yet before he makes the magic top ten, Peter set to work with a vengeance during 1989 and duly qualified for the 1990 show through the AIT system.

Still only twenty in 1989, he was eligible to ride in that year's Young Riders European Championships at Stoneleigh and looked to have a good chance of scoring a record hat-trick of

Peter found no problem in switching from ponies to horses. Here he is seen partnering PPD at Wembley

Under-21 individual gold medals. The British squad as a whole was not as strong as in the past and finished way down the team ratings. But Peter kept the flag flying by once again jumping a double clear round in the Nations Cup, which took him comfortably through to the individual final. One fence down deprived him of a third title, but in a jump-off for the lesser medals he won the bronze. During the summer he also began acquiring valuable experience with senior teams abroad.

The regard in which he is held by his elders is reflected in the fact that during that year senior team manager Ronnie Massarella invited Peter to ride for him. He made the move to Ronnie's home near Laughton, in South Yorkshire, immediately after the Horse of the Year Show, taking with him Jay's Way and Leamlara. In addition to these two tried and trusted partners he now has the ride on both novices and more experienced horses for Ronnie.

During all the years that he was too young to hold an HGV licence, it was his mother he had to thank for keeping the show on the road. Indeed, Peter's has been very much a family success story, with Diana taking the role of chief box driver and secretary and his younger sister Caroline acting as groom. 'Now we're redundant,' his mother said with a laugh after he had moved to Yorkshire. 'but we've always been a close family and we shall still be at shows to support him.'

In his rare spare time – some of the best moments are during shows abroad – Peter enjoys a game of golf. But leisure is something of a luxury, and for the moment he is content to devote most of his time to the one thing that matters most to him: getting to the top and making a living out of show jumping.

Career Highlights

1983 Pony European Championships, team gold medal (Mr Punch)
1984 Pony European Championships, individual gold and team silver medals (Foxlynch Little John)
1985 Pony European Championships, team gold and individual silver medals (Foxlynch Little John)
      Leading Junior Show Jumper of the Year, Wembley
1987 Junior European Championships, individual gold medal (Jay's Way)
      Young Rider of the Year, Wembley (PPD)
1989 Young Riders European Championships, individual bronze medal (Jay's Way)

Marie Edgar

ARIE EDGAR TOOK THE SENIOR JUMPING WORLD by storm at Royal Windsor in 1988 when, at the age of just seventeen, she won five classes, including the Grand Prix. It was her first ever Grand Prix appearance and the cool assurance with which she rode Everest Surething to victory over such seasoned campaigners as Sue Pountain, Annette Lewis, Graham Fletcher and her own Everest team-mate Emma-Jane Mac demonstrated that here, without any shadow of doubt, was a future international star.

With Ted Edgar for a father and David Broome's sister Liz for a mother, it is scarcely surprising that Marie should have settled on a career with horses very early in her young life. Ted, the son of a Warwickshire farmer and a keen rider to hounds, was a big winner in show classes, point-to-points and show jumping before giving up competitive riding in 1980 to become a full-time trainer. Liz, of course, still competes with great success at national and international level.

Marie, who was born on 28 February 1971, was given her first pony by her grandfather, Fred Broome, when she was two. His name was Jewel and he was, not surprisingly considering her grandfather's enthusiasm for his local ponies, Welsh. It was not

Marie Edgar, the first rider to win two Junior European titles, riding Surething

long before Marie was learning to handle and look after him and, in time, to ride round the fields at home, chiefly under the supervision of her nanny. By the time of her seventh birthday, Liz and Ted had bought her two nice jumping ponies, Bali and Franco. When she started competing on the junior circuit with them she was rarely out of the money.

From that time on, her ambition was to become a show jumper. Other children's equestrian activities, such as gymkhana games, did not interest her; she was always going to jump, and to do it professionally. She did not enjoy school, and left just as soon as she could. The only further education she undertook was a typing course because 'I thought it would come in useful.' But horses are now her full-time preoccupation.

Marie has inherited some of her mother's talent and some of her father's. Like Liz she has the ability to get horses jumping in a controlled, beautifully balanced manner, but her style is in some ways more reminiscent of her father, being more forceful and aggressive than her mother's. And she has also inherited something of her father's volatile temperament.

Although she made the transition from ponies to horses with no apparent problems, she admits to not being the bravest of riders and is sensibly working her way through Young Riders en route to what she clearly feels is the daunting prospect of senior Grands Prix. But all along the line she has taken on the best riders of her age in Europe and beaten them.

Riding Invincible Lad, the horse that her father sold on to Nigel Coupe's family a few months later, she finished fifth in her first Junior European Championship at Mons in Belgium in 1987. The victor on that occasion was Peter Murphy, two years her senior. After sweeping the board at Windsor the following spring she announced that her immediate ambition was to take the Junior European title at Bourg-en-Bresse in France two months later. And that is exactly what she did, jumping the only double clear round with her impressive young grey gelding Surething. She also collected a team silver medal.

The Junior European Championships, first run for teams in 1952 and for teams and individuals since 1959, are the oldest of the official FEI championships, and have over the years been won by many riders who have gone on to top international honours, among them Ann Moore, Markus Fuchs, Debbie Johnsey, Nick Skelton, Eric Navet and Gillian Greenwood. Prior to 1989 no one had won the individual championship twice, but Marie embarked on that season determined to retain her title, and on 2 July at Neunen, in Holland, she achieved her ambition, again riding Surething. One of only two riders to complete the two rounds faultlessly, she produced the faster clear in the jump-off to relegate

Marie has clearly inherited her mother's gift for getting horses jumping in a rhythmic, balanced way. Here she is partnering Minka

Sven Wienfort of the Federal Republic of Germany to the runner-up position. Sven had also taken the silver medal the previous year. With a clear round and 4 faults in the Nations Cup, Marie also contributed to victory in the team championship, the first time Britain had won the team gold since 1981.

At home Marie and Surething won the two major young rider titles at the 1988 Horse of the Year Show, the Oakley Coachbuilders Young Rider of the Year and the Brown Group National 21 Championship. Proving that she is by no means a one-horse rider, she also took third place in the Young Rider of the Year with the Countess of Inchcape's Everest Minka.

At the Mechelen international show in Belgium at the end of the year she was consistently in the money with Minka and t'Soulaiky, the horse previously ridden by Ferdi Tyteca. Her prize for being leading young rider of the show was original, to say the least: her weight in Coca Cola. (She also received a slightly odd prize for her second Junior European title: a set of hi-fi equipment – minus the speakers!)

In 1989 Marie narrowly missed winning the two Wembley young rider championships for a second time. On this occasion she got two horses through to the jump-off of each event. She finished second in the Young Rider of the Year on Everest Unique, another good horse owned by the Countess of Inchcape with whom Marie had won the National Grade C Championship the day before, and fourth on Surething. In the National 21 she was second on Minka and fourth again on Surething. Ironically, she was defeated in both classes by Nigel Coupe on her old partner Invincible Lad. Understandably, she prefers not to talk about her father's decision to sell that horse to her rival!

With Minka she took a very creditable third place in the valuable Everest Championship behind Michael Whitaker on Next Tees Hanauer and Emma-Jane Mac on Everest Oyster, and finished the show as the eighth highest money-winning rider, with £5649 to her credit. At Olympia in December she won the Vauxhall Young Show Jumper of the Future Award on Unique. Normally the riders who qualify for the final of this nationwide championship cannot compete in the international competitions at the show, but it is a tradition that current British holders of the Junior or Young Riders' European title are invited to take part in the afternoon classes. Marie wasted no time in accepting the challenge, and rounded off the season in great style by winning the Cognac Courvoisier Christmas Pudding Stakes on Minka, beating none other than her mother on Everest Asher. By the end of the year Marie was in eleventh place on the riders' computer ranking list, having overtaken her mother.

Since show jumping these days is very much a year-round sport, Marie's social life, like that of other young riders, tends to revolve around the horse world. When she does have the leisure she enjoys swimming – the Edgars have their own pool – but she says she has little time for other hobbies.

With her determined, accurate style of riding, deadly eye against the clock and compulsion to win, Marie looks destined for stardom. Ronnie Massarella, manager of the senior team, has no doubts that she is going to become a top international rider. 'With the expertise she has backing her and her own natural talent, she is a great prospect for the future. She is an out-and-out winner, and that's the greatest gift of all.'

Career Highlights

1988   Junior European Championships, individual gold and
            team silver medals (Surething)
        Windsor Grand Prix (Surething)
        Young Rider of the Year (Surething)
        National 21 Championship (Surething)
1989   Junior European Championships, individual and team
            gold medals (Surething)
        Young Show Jumper of the Future Award (Unique)